FANTASY
ENCYCLOPEDIA

FANTASY
ENCYCLOPEDIA

JUDY ALLEN

KINGFISHER
BOSTON

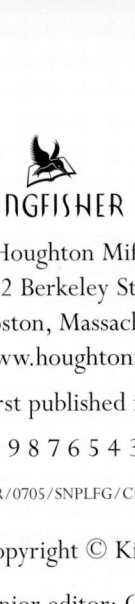

KINGFISHER

a Houghton Mifflin Company imprint
222 Berkeley Street
Boston, Massachusetts 02116
www.houghtonmifflinbooks.com

First published in 2005

10 9 8 7 6 5 4 3 2 1

1TR/0705/SNPLFG/CLSN(CLSN)/140MA/C

Senior editor: Carron Brown
Coordinating editor: Caitlin Doyle
Senior designer: Jane Tassie
Picture research manager: Cee Weston-Baker
DTP manager: Nicky Studdart
DTP operator: Primrose Burton
Senior production controller: Lindsey Scott
Artwork archivist: Wendy Allison
Proofreaders: Sheila Clewley, Caitlin Doyle,
  Essie Cousins
Additional text and indexer: Carron Brown

Judy Allen's web site: www.judyallen.co.uk

The publisher cannot be held responsible
for changes in web site addresses or content.

LIBRARY OF CONGRESS CATALOGING-IN-
PUBLICATION DATA
Allen, Judy.
Fantasy encyclopedia/Judy Allen.—1st ed.
    p. cm.
Includes index.
1. Fairies—Encyclopedias, Juvenile. 2.
Animals, Mythical—Encyclopedias, Juvenile.
I. Title.
GR549.A45 2005
398.4'03—cd22   2004029475

ISBN 0-7534-5847-0
ISBN 978-07534-5847-1

Printed in China

Special thanks
*The author and publisher would like
to thank John Howe and Tamlyn Francis
for all of their help and enthusiasm.*

Contents

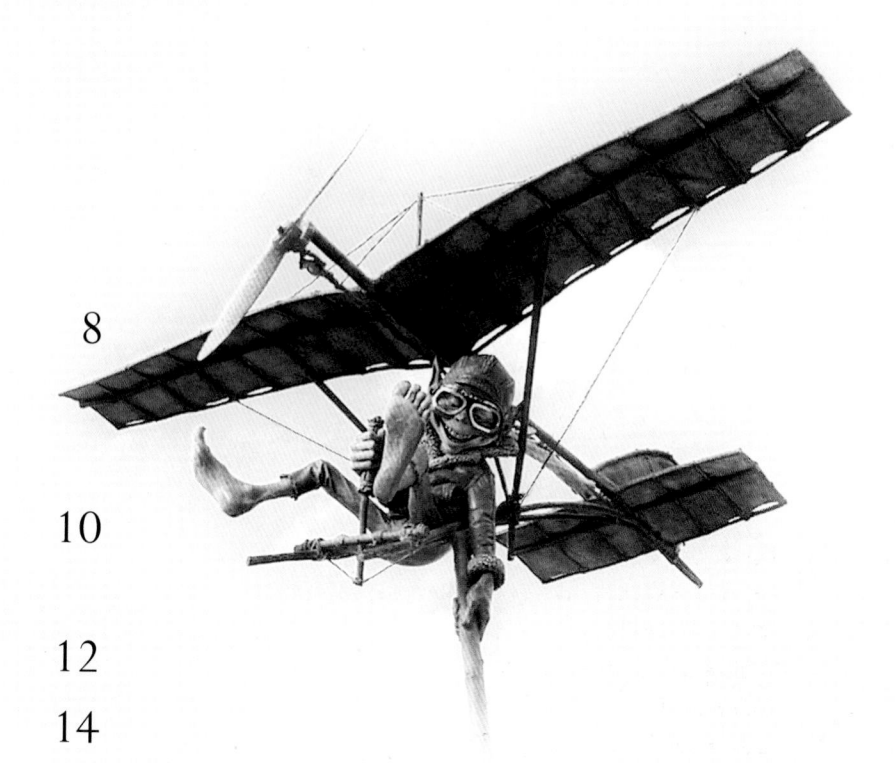

Foreword

Warning: the creatures in this book are real.
Well okay, maybe not real physically—
don't expect to find a bunyip in your
bathtub or a hobgoblin under your bed. If you comb
the woods for a Sasquatch, the most you'll find is a
tuft of hair caught on a twig—and that might belong
to anything. But make no mistake. They're real, all right.
And when you read their stories, they'll come to you.

I should know. I left a door to my imagination open when
I was very young, and they all got in. They're still there now: fairies,
dragons, vampires, genies—all jostling for a position inside my head.

Fantasy sometimes scared me, but it mostly made me soar. Between the
ages of seven and ten I was often ill and spent a lot of time in bed. Once I
was home from school for a whole term. Reading was all I could do, and I
read a lot. Not stories about real life—I wanted escape. I wanted things
that took me away from my dull, little room and my wheezing chest.
I wanted myths and monsters; I wanted flying horses to carry me
to distant lands. And fantasy obliged.

Pegasus came and whisked me away—to the Cyclops' cave, to the sorcerous
palaces of Arabia, to Baba Yaga's terrifying forest hut. I sought great treasures,
vast knowledge, true love, and eternal life. I met many of the creatures in this
book and learned how to deal with them. Some should be befriended (despite
their strangeness), while others can be tamed. With some you can bargain; the
very worst must be fought and destroyed. There are rules for each one, and they

are worth knowing. Taken together, they draw on all our endurance, courage, intelligence, and compassion—the finest qualities that make us human.

I got better. I went back to school. I grew up. Got a job. But the wonders I had seen stayed with me—I glimpsed them as I sat at my desk or walked through crowded London streets. And in the end I couldn't ignore their call. I began writing my own stories, with my own versions of genies, imps, water spirits, and dragons . . . This is how the creatures of fantasy have survived for thousands of years—passing from one person to another, always evolving, always changing. And now they're heading your way too.

Let this book be your guide—the key to their mysteries. Open it on any page, and you'll find something to enchant you. It describes the shadowy, slippery inhabitants of fantasy and suggests where you might find them; even better, it tells you the rules of engagement—silver bullets and all.

This extraordinary encyclopedia is a portal to another world. Step on through and be amazed!

Jonathan Stroud,
author of The Bartimaeus Trilogy

What is fantasy?

Defining the word "fantasy" is like catching fog in a fishing net. Fantasy is fluid and ever-changing, with no fixed boundaries. Its worlds drift in and out of our world, always closeby, but often only visible to the imagination. Within it are myths, legends, fables, and folklore, although these also exist outside of it. Fantasy includes magic—both the natural enchantment of elves, fairies, and spirit beings, and the more scientific magic used by human magicians. Trying to define fantasy by its opposite does not help either. The opposite of fantasy is reality—yet to say that fantasy is unreal is to imply that it does not exist, and clearly it does. Certainly between the covers of this book each fabulous beast, each magical being, every ghost and spirit and vampire exists, with its own energy and its own power. Outside the book—readers must decide for themselves.

The very forms of the creatures and beings within fantasy are changeable. Many are shape-shifters: djinn who can become smoke or mist; men who can turn into wolves; vampires who can just as easily have the bodies of bats as of humans; forest spirits who may be as tall as the tallest tree or as small as a blade of grass. And many of them have different aspects. One of these is the triple goddess who can appear as a young girl, a grown woman, or an aged

hag, and who can be innocent or nurturing or vengeful, depending
on her mood. Another is the dragon of the East, who can as easily bring
the rain that makes plants grow as the rain that causes devastating floods.

Arranging the various beings and creatures into groups for the sake of
this book was difficult. They watch as you write about them—looming and
hovering—and you know they do not like to be pinned down and trapped.

In the end decisions had to be made, and here they
are—although I have to say that each time I close the
book and then open it up again, I half expect to find
the dragons and giant birds have flown away, and
the rest have drifted onto different pages.

Judy Allen

NOTE TO READERS
This book includes historical creatures
of fantasy from folklore, legends, and fables.
Book and movie panels throughout will guide
you to fictional characters, such as hobbits,
and fictional worlds such as Narnia.

Few humans see fairies or hear
their music, but many find fairy
rings of dark grass, scattered with
toadstools, left by their dancing feet.

CHAPTER ONE

The Little People

Elves, fairies, dwarves, goblins, and their kind have been written about and spoken of in every part of the world for hundreds of years. They have many names in many different languages, but they prefer to be called The Strangers, The Good Neighbors, or The Little People. They can be gentle and generous or dark and dangerous—but even the friendliest are unreliable.

Elves and fairies

Elves have been known to humans for more than 2,000 years. They are much older than fairies. In medieval Europe a fairy was a human woman with magical powers. It was a few hundred years before the word "fairy" was also used to describe elves. The image of fairies with gauzy wings did not appear until the late A.D. 1700s. Now, either the words "elves" or "fairies" are used for the Little People of the woods and fields.

Some elves are tiny, others are tall, and elfin women can even occasionally seem human. Seen from behind though, they have no backs and are hollow, like a hollow tree.

14

DIFFERENT FAIRIES

Trooping fairies, such as the Patu-Paiarehe of the Maori
of New Zealand, live in trees and appear in mists. Like elves
everywhere, they love music and dancing. They will sometimes
teach humans to work magic, but if they call from far away,
any humans who follow risk becoming lost in the woods.

Some fairies are solitary such as leprechauns. They are
very rich, and humans may try to persuade a leprechaun
to lead the way across meadows and marshes to his
secret stash of gold. He will always trick them into
looking away, when he will then vanish, leaving
them lost, bewildered, and with no treasure.

*The leprechaun is the
fairy shoemaker of
Ireland whose tapping
hammer gives away
his presence.*

When blackberry picking, always leave a few for the Little People.

FAIRIES AND HUMANS

In stories good fairies bring blessings and help, although
there are often conditions attached. Cinderella must be
home by midnight or her beautiful dress will turn to rags.
A farmer who is paid by the fairies for help or provisions
must not look at the money until he gets home or it will
turn into dead leaves. Then again, he may be paid in dead
leaves that will turn into gold when he reaches home.

Pixies, who are tiny, always young, and dressed in
green, will help humans—especially if they are poor
or are being mistreated by others. However, they can be
tricky and mischievous if they are annoyed or not properly
rewarded. In fact, to be "pixie led" means to be lost.

Many Little People appreciate a tribute or a gift.
Traditionally people put out a little bread from a new
loaf or, when the cows are being milked, allow a little
milk to run onto the ground for the Little People to take.

FAIRIES IN BOOKS AND MOVIES

📖 *The Complete Book of the
Flower Fairies*
Cicely Mary Barker

📖 *Peter Pan*
J. M. Barrie

📖 *The Little People: Stories of Fairies,
Pixies, and Other Small Folk*
Neil Philip

🎬 *Hook* (1991)

🎬 *The Last Leprechaun* (1998)

Traps and tricks

In early folklore elves—although beautiful and sometimes generous—are treated with nervous respect. They are intrigued by humans, but being quick, small, and supernatural, they can always outwit them. Elves will steal cows, bread, milk—and even a baby, who they raise as their own, leaving a changeling, or elf-child, in its place.

KIDNAP!

Elvish women are sometimes attracted to young mortal men and may lure them into a fairy ring, from which it is difficult to escape. It is also the case that when elves have taken a human baby, they may try to kidnap a mortal woman to take care of the child.

TIME IN FAIRYLAND

It is said to be possible for mortal men and women to spend time in fairyland and still get home safely—but only if they do not eat or drink anything while they are there. A single mouthful of fairy food, and a mortal is the fairies' forever.

People who escape from fairyland find that time is different there than it is in their own world—one hour in fairyland can be many years in human time.

Flint arrowheads were once believed to be elf shot— the spent weapons of elves, whose victims would incur illness or disability.

In their more playful moments elves spend the night twisting the hair of humans or the manes of horses, and the tangles they leave are known as elf locks.

LIGHT AND DARK ELVES

The light elves live in the air or in trees and are usually kind. The dark elves, who live underground, are inclined to play malicious tricks and can make people sick just by breathing on them.

All elves have the power to use "glamour" or enchantment to make themselves invisible. A fairy market can be seen from a distance easily, but disappears when a human gets close. Walk through it and you will be jostled and bumped as you would if you walked unseeing through a human market. Once you get home, you are likely to discover that you have become sick or injured.

Elves enjoy teasing humans and laugh at their confusion.

TRICKSTERS

In German one word for nightmare is *alpdrücken*, which translates as "elf pressure," because it was thought that elves would sit on their victims' chests all night.

The music of the Elf King, played on a fiddle, can sometimes be heard seeping up through the ground. If a human plays the same tune, anyone and anything that hears it will be forced to dance until the poor fiddler can play the tune backward or someone can cut the fiddle strings.

ELVES IN BOOKS AND MOVIES

📖 *Elf Hill*
Hans Christian Andersen

📖 *The Various*
Steve Augarde

📖 *The Changeling*
Malachy Doyle

🎬 *Elf* (2003)

Celebrated fairies

The most celebrated fairies are found in literature—in folktales and fairy tales, in French medieval romances, and in some of Shakespeare's plays. Some have names—including Oberon, Titania, and Puck. Others are known only by their title—the Tooth Fairy, who leaves money in exchange for lost teeth, or the fairy godmother, who brings good fortune and grants wishes.

Robin Goodfellow—also known as Puck—is the son of Oberon, King of the Fairies, and a mortal woman. His father gave him the power to shape-shift, create illusions, and cast spells. He is the most mischievous of the hobgoblins and the best at leading travelers astray.

OBERON AND TITANIA

Oberon, King of the Fairies, first appeared in a French Romantic poem, *Huon de Bordeaux*, written in the A.D. 1200s or 1300s. The inspiration for Oberon probably came from Germany and tales of the Dwarf King Elberich or Albrich.

Later, in the 1500s, Oberon and his queen, Titania, appeared in *A Midsummer Night's Dream*—a play by William Shakespeare (1564–1616). In Shakespeare's time fairies were believed to be the same as the nymphs who followed the Roman moon goddess Diana, and Titania is another name for Diana. Although this fairy king and queen are invented beings, everything they do follows elvish tradition.

Not all sightings of fairies are genuine. In 1917 in the village of Cottingley, England, two children created fake photographs of themselves with fairies. They convinced many adults, including the writer of the Sherlock Holmes detective novels, Sir Arthur Conan Doyle (1859–1930). It was not until they were old women that one of them finally confessed.

**CELEBRATED FAIRIES IN
BOOKS AND MOVIES**

📖 *Cinderella*
Charles Perrault

📖 *A Midsummer Night's Dream*
William Shakespeare

🎥 *FairyTale: A True Story* (1997)

🎥 *Shrek 2* (2004)

🎥 *Sleeping Beauty* (1959)

FAIRY GODMOTHERS

They appear in Greek and Roman mythology as the Fates. In Scandinavian mythology they are Norns or Nornir. There are three of them, and some say that they plan human destiny, while others say that they simply foretell it. Certainly they spin out the thread of each human life, and when they cut the thread, that life ends.

After much retelling of the Norns myths the women were described as fairies who visit each newborn baby and announce what the future holds for that child. Then came the belief that they brought gifts to the child at birth—not material things, but good fortune, talents, and abilities. They became known as fairy godmothers, and in some tales there are seven of them, or 12, or even more.

As they changed through the years, so did their behavior—Cinderella was not a baby but a young woman when her fairy godmother first came to her assistance.

The fairies from fiction almost always carry wands. The Christmas Tree Fairy or a fairy godmother (shown here in a 1940s picture) would seem powerless without this important piece of magical equipment. Traditional elves and fairies rarely, if ever, use such things.

19

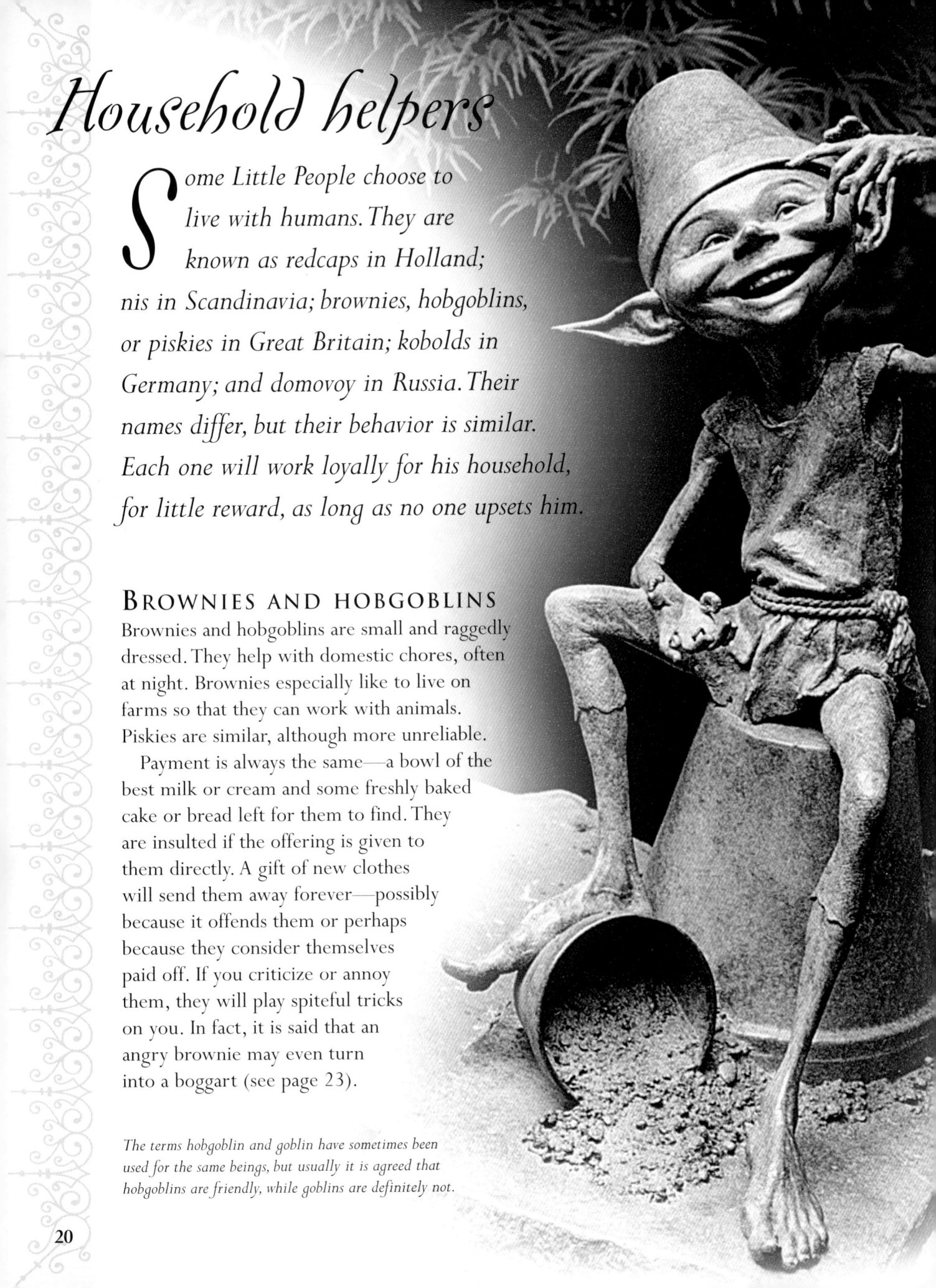

Household helpers

Some Little People choose to live with humans. They are known as redcaps in Holland; nis in Scandinavia; brownies, hobgoblins, or piskies in Great Britain; kobolds in Germany; and domovoy in Russia. Their names differ, but their behavior is similar. Each one will work loyally for his household, for little reward, as long as no one upsets him.

BROWNIES AND HOBGOBLINS

Brownies and hobgoblins are small and raggedly dressed. They help with domestic chores, often at night. Brownies especially like to live on farms so that they can work with animals. Piskies are similar, although more unreliable.

Payment is always the same—a bowl of the best milk or cream and some freshly baked cake or bread left for them to find. They are insulted if the offering is given to them directly. A gift of new clothes will send them away forever—possibly because it offends them or perhaps because they consider themselves paid off. If you criticize or annoy them, they will play spiteful tricks on you. In fact, it is said that an angry brownie may even turn into a boggart (see page 23).

The terms hobgoblin and goblin have sometimes been used for the same beings, but usually it is agreed that hobgoblins are friendly, while goblins are definitely not.

DOMOVOY

The domovoy looks like an old, gray-bearded man wearing a gray robe or a red shirt. He lives with a family, and if that family moves to a new house, he will go with them. They should put a slice of bread under the stove in the new house in order to welcome him in. A domovoy's work should always be appreciated, and he must only be referred to as "Himself" or "Grandfather." He dislikes bad language. If he is really annoyed, he will burn the house down, but usually he will protect his chosen family and make himself useful.

Kobolds will sweep the floor, wash dishes, and discover the secret places where the hens have laid their eggs.

ORIGINS OF LITTLE PEOPLE

These helpful beings do not all live in houses. Some prefer barns or outhouses, caves, or the hollow hearts of huge trees. This fits in with a theory that all elvish folk are members of an early race of people who were driven from their lands by newcomers. This would explain their need to be respected, even though they must rely on the stronger race for food. Another theory says that these Little People are the spirits of dead ancestors. Many, though, choose to believe that they are completely separate from humanity and are truly supernatural beings, dressed in brown or green, often with red caps, and always with magical powers.

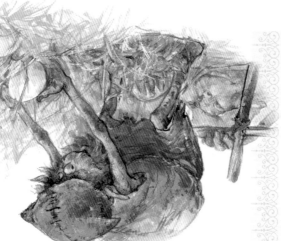

The domovoy lives behind the stove and, like the redcap, is good at lighting hearth fires. Creaks and noises at night are the sounds of the domovoy finishing off the household chores.

HOUSEHOLD HELPERS IN BOOKS AND MOVIES

📖 *The Elves and the Shoemaker* — The Brothers Grimm

📖 *The Field Guide (The Spiderwick Chronicles)* — Tony DiTerlizzi and Holly Black

🎬 *Harry Potter and the Chamber of Secrets* (2002)

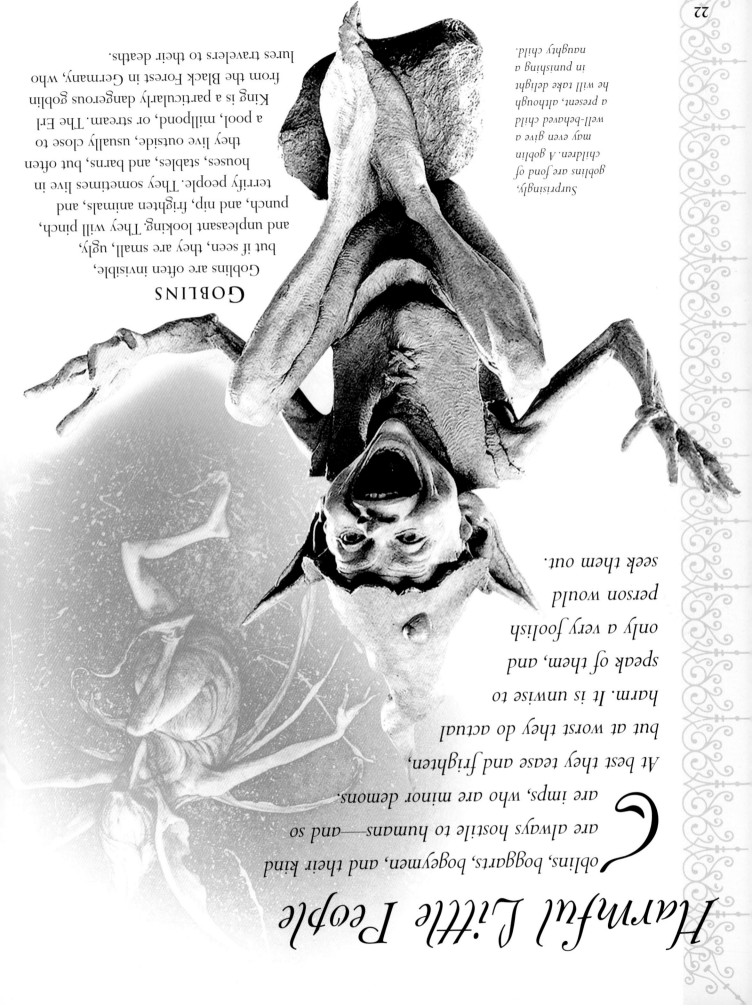

Harmful Little People

oblins, boggarts, bogeymen, and their kind are always hostile to humans—and so are imps, who are minor demons.

At best they tease and frighten, but at worst they do actual harm. It is unwise to speak of them, and only a very foolish person would seek them out.

GOBLINS

Goblins are often invisible, but if seen, they are small, ugly, and unpleasant looking. They will pinch, punch, and nip, frighten animals, and terrify people. They sometimes live in houses, stables, and barns, but often they live outside, usually close to a pool, millpond, or stream. The Erl King is a particularly dangerous goblin from the Black Forest in Germany, who lures travelers to their deaths.

Surprisingly, goblins are fond of children. A goblin may even give a well-behaved child a present, although he will take delight in punishing a naughty child.

DREADFUL DANCERS

Northern France has the White Ladies— sometimes known as fées—who wait near bridges after dark until a lone man passes by. The White Lady will ask him to dance with her. If he accepts, she will release him at the end of the dance, and he will be safe. If he refuses, she will throw him over the bridge or set her pet owls and cats on him.

Goblins have never been known to be helpful, but the Tokoloshi of South Africa does useful work around the house. However, he is dangerous because he works for a witch or a sorcerer who will send him to torment or attack his victims. He will not harm a child though, even if he is ordered to do so.

It is possible to keep these Little People at bay. A horseshoe hung over a door will prevent them from entering. A four-leafed clover does not only grant wishes, it also protects its owner from goblin attacks.

BOGGART AND BOGEYMAN

The boggart enjoys scaring people. Outside he may follow them in lonely places after dark; inside he will behave like a noisy poltergeist (see pages 130–131). The bogeyman has many names, including Boggelman in Germany, Bubak in Bohemia, and Bocan in Ireland. He is a malicious goblin, covered in black hair, who can be dangerous but is more often just spiteful. Fortunately these creatures are not very intelligent and can often be outwitted.

HARMFUL LITTLE PEOPLE IN BOOKS AND MOVIES

📖 *The Boggart*
Susan Cooper

📖 *The Goblin Companion*
Brian Froud and Terry Jones

📖 *The Princess and the Goblin*
George MacDonald

🎬 *Labyrinth* (1986)

Underground

Dwarves live underground and look like small, elderly, bearded men, with lined faces, gnarled hands, and bright eyes. Just as elves are usually young, it seems that dwarves are almost always old. Many of them are miners and skilled metalworkers, and their underground homes are full of handcrafted treasures and precious stones.

The bluecap appears in mines as a small, blue flame. If treated with respect, bluecaps will lead miners to rich veins of ore or coal and forewarn them of danger, just as the knockers and wichtlein do.

THUMPERS AND LITTLE WIGHTS

In the old tin mines in Cornwall, England, the coal mines in Wales, and throughout the working mines of northern Europe, dwarves are called thumpers or knockers because they communicate with humans by rapping and banging on the mine walls. Repeated knocking in one place means that there is a rich seam to be mined there. Heavy digging and pounding noises warn of danger from flood or falling roofs. In Germany, where they are called wichtlein, or little wights, three distinct knocks foretell the death of a miner.

Dwarves are usually helpful and are believed to bring good fortune. However, it is wise to leave food out for them and never to swear or even to whistle when they are around.

The household elves called kobolds (see page 21) also work in mines, but there they are mischievous and likely to throw stones.

DWARVES IN BOOKS AND MOVIES

📖 *Snow White and the Seven Dwarves*
The Brothers Grimm

📖 *Artemis Fowl: The Seventh Dwarf*
Eoin Colfer

📖 *The Hobbit*
J. R. R. Tolkien

📖 *The Lord of the Rings*
J. R. R. Tolkien

🎬 *Time Bandits* (1981)

BARBEGAZI

The barbegazi are dwarves who live in the Alps in France and Switzerland. Their name comes from the French *barbes glacées*, which means "frozen beards." Their white fur clothes—as well as the icicles in their hair and beards—make them very difficult to see in the winter. In the summer they hibernate in caves and tunnels in the rocks and do not come out until the first snowfall. Their greatest excitement is surfing on avalanches, although they will give low whistling cries to warn humans of the danger and will do their best to dig humans out if they become trapped.

ULDRA

The dwarves who live within the Arctic Circle, in the far north of Norway, Sweden, Finland, and Russia are called uldra. Like the barbegazi, they hibernate underground in the summer. The uldra emerge on winter nights to care for the reindeer and moose that graze on the lichen and moss through the bleak months. They never leave their burrows in daylight because it dazzles them. Although the uldra are not unfriendly to humans, they will become enraged if reindeer herdsmen accidentally set up their temporary tents over the narrow openings of their burrows.

Barbegazi have huge feet that enable them to run across soft snow and ski down steep slopes.

25

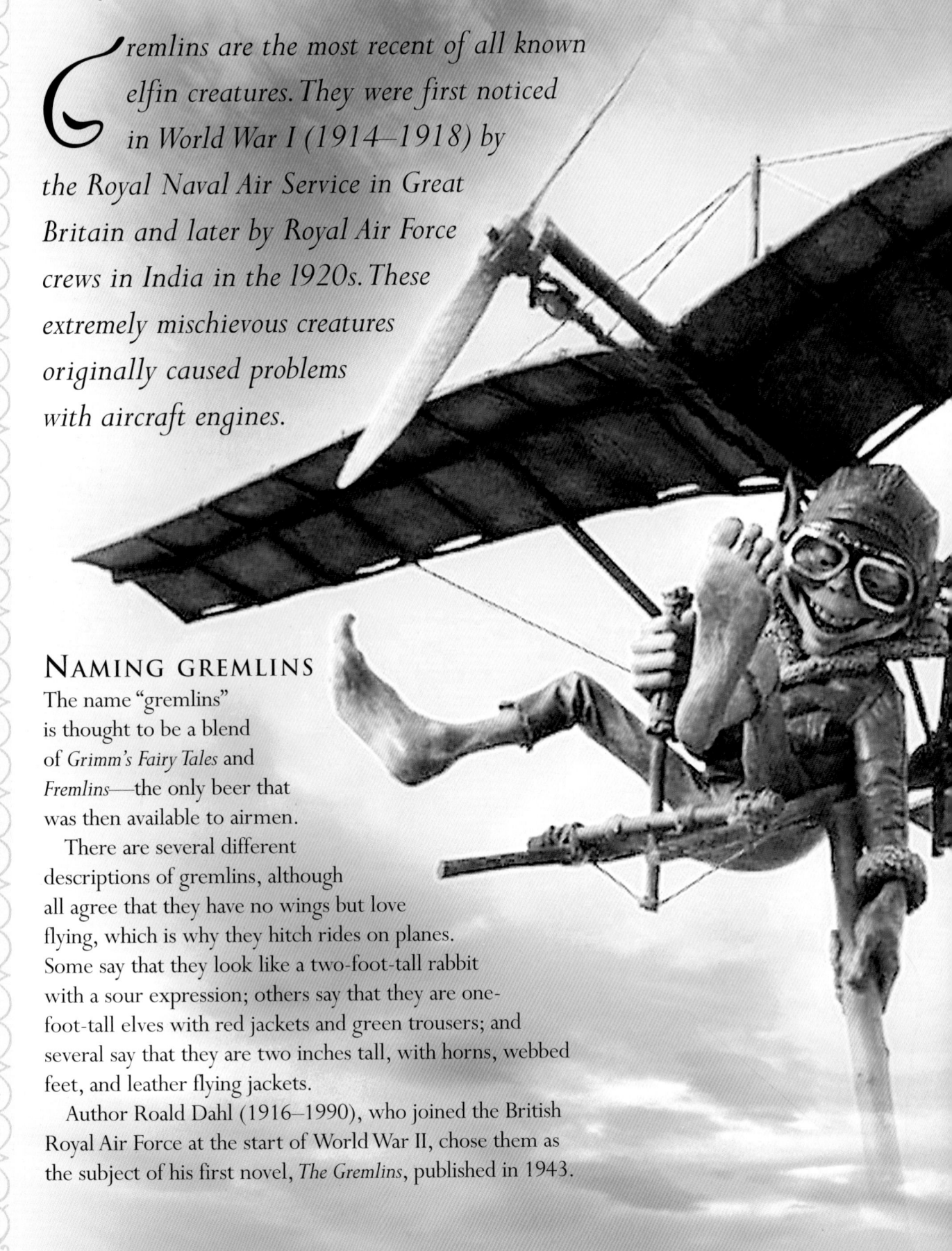

Gremlins

Gremlins are the most recent of all known elfin creatures. They were first noticed in *World War I (1914–1918)* by the Royal Naval Air Service in Great Britain and later by Royal Air Force crews in India in the 1920s. These extremely mischievous creatures originally caused problems with aircraft engines.

NAMING GREMLINS

The name "gremlins" is thought to be a blend of *Grimm's Fairy Tales* and *Fremlins*—the only beer that was then available to airmen.

There are several different descriptions of gremlins, although all agree that they have no wings but love flying, which is why they hitch rides on planes. Some say that they look like a two-foot-tall rabbit with a sour expression; others say that they are one-foot-tall elves with red jackets and green trousers; and several say that they are two inches tall, with horns, webbed feet, and leather flying jackets.

Author Roald Dahl (1916–1990), who joined the British Royal Air Force at the start of World War II, chose them as the subject of his first novel, *The Gremlins*, published in 1943.

GREMLINS IN BOOKS

📖 *Electric Girl*
Michael Brennan

📖 *Troll Fell*
Katherine Langrish

📖 *The Greedy Gremlin*
Tracey West

📖 Sadly, Roald Dahl's novel
The Gremlins is out of print and
so cannot be bought in bookstores.

Grimm's Fairy Tales
is a collection of folktales
and fairy stories gathered
together by two German
brothers, Jacob Grimm
(1785–1863) and Wilhelm
Grimm (1786–1859),
in the early 1800s.

GREMLIN BEHAVIOR

The World War I gremlins lived in burrows
at the edges of airfields. Once on a plane, they
were able to cause any one of the controls to
malfunction or fail completely. They would
also interfere with the wireless radio and
drink the fuel. The really powerful ones could
rearrange the stars in the sky to mislead the
navigator. Ground-based gremlins could cause
an entire airfield to rise or sink just as a plane
was coming in to land.

Nowadays, gremlins have managed to
creep into almost everything mechanical or
electronic. They can be blamed for countless
problems, from cars refusing to start to
computers crashing or behaving strangely.

There is no record of
a gremlin actually flying
any type of plane, but it
seems likely (because of
their fascination with
planes) that this was
their ultimate ambition.

CHAPTER TWO

Elementals and nature spirits

Elementals are the spirits of the individual elements that combine to make up all things. Nature spirits— genius loci *in Latin*—are the spirits or guardians of specific places. Every glade, stream, and pool, as well as every mountain, forest, and tree, has its own spirit, which is both its life force and its protector.

Elementals

Everything is made up of a mixture of elements in different amounts. In ancient Chinese and Eastern teachings there are five elements—earth, fire, metal, water, and wood—each one with its symbolic creature or elemental. Earth is represented by a yellow phoenix; fire by a red pheasant; metal by a white tiger; water by a black turtle, sometimes combined with a serpent; and wood by a green dragon.

THE FOUR ELEMENTALS

It is thought that a Sicilian philosopher named Empedocles (c. 490–430 B.C.) first developed the idea of only four elements: earth, air, fire, and water. Certainly Plato (c. 428–348 B.C.) and Aristotle (385–322 B.C.) accepted it as a scientific fact. The belief that everything was made up of just four ingredients convinced some alchemists that it would be possible to change one into another—and many of them attempted to transform ordinary metal into gold.

EARTH ELEMENTALS

Gnomes belong to the earth. The earth is where they live, and into the earth is where they vanish. Gnomes are ancient and dark and often dressed in a monk's habit. Usually hunched and small, they can shape-shift into giants at will.

Gnomes are not at all like garden gnomes, who are really dwarves, a mistake that began in early fairy tales.

30

FIRE ELEMENTALS

Salamanders are symbols of fire.
Some believed that their skin was so
cold that it could put fire out; others
believed that they chose to live in flames and
could even strengthen them. However, these
were the Salamanders of fantasy. In reality
there are several types of these amphibious
lizards, and none of them—not even
the black and gold European fire
salamander—can survive flames.

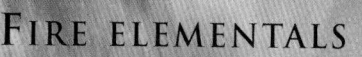

ELEMENTALS IN BOOKS AND MOVIES

📖 *The Tears of the Salamander*
Peter Dickinson

📖 *The Ragwitch*
Garth Nix

🎥 *Fantasia* (1940)

AIR ELEMENTALS

Sylphs are the light, ethereal spirits of the air.
Like the gnomes and the Undines, they were
first named by Paracelcus (A.D. 1493–1541),
a physician and alchemist, whose real name
was Theophrastus Bombastus von Hohenheim.
He named himself "Paracelcus," which meant
"greater than Celcus," a famous Roman
authority on medicine.

WATER ELEMENTALS

Undines, or Nereids, are water elementals.
They are rarely seen, although they may
sometimes become visible drifting in the
spray from waterfalls or the mist that rises
from the surface of water at dawn or dusk.

Nymphs

Nymphs are nature spirits who take the form of young and beautiful women. They are known in many different countries and cultures. There are several main groups—Oceanids of the ocean; Nereids of the sea; Naiads of springs, streams, and rivers; Oreads of the mountains; Dryads of woods and forests; and Hamadryads of individual trees.

TREE NYMPHS

The Dryads are daughters of Zeus—the greatest of the Greek gods. They are not immortal, but they can live for many, many years—as long as the forests or woods that they inhabit. They are especially fond of oak trees and often wear garlands made of oak leaves. Although they are gentle and usually have no problem with humans, they will do their best to protect their trees. If a wood or forest is threatened, the Dryads will join together and use all their power to make it a very frightening place for those who plan to cut it down. They are rarely seen, although humans who are still and quiet may glimpse them moving among their trees. The Hamadryads do not move—each one is always a part of her own tree, and she will live only as long as the tree itself.

WATER NYMPHS

There are believed to be 50 sea nymphs, known as Nereids—daughters of Nereus, the wise old man of the sea. They share their name with the water elementals. The sea that they live in is the Mediterranean and, unlike the Sirens (see pages 72–73), they are helpful to those who sail across it.

The nymphs who live in the wide oceans are called Oceanids, while the Naiads are the spirits of running water, from springs and streams to great rivers.

ARTEMIS

All the nymphs, as well as the mountain Oreads, the tree nymphs, and the rest, follow the Greek goddess Artemis—who is also called Diana in Roman mythology. She is a moon goddess and a mother goddess, associated with the countryside and with tree worship. She is a huntress, but she is also the protector of women as they give birth, of children, and of all young animals.

NYMPHS IN BOOKS

📖 *Apollo & Daphne: Masterpieces of Greek Mythology*
Antonia Barber (Narrator)

📖 *The Chronicles of Narnia*
C. S. Lewis

THE STORY OF DAPHNE

Many of the nymphs have their own stories, and the Greek tale of Daphne is one of the best known. She was the daughter of a river god named Peneus and was, like all nymphs, beautiful. The sun god Apollo fell in love with her, but Daphne did not love him, and she ran away. He chased her and caught her. She called out for help to Mother Earth, Gaea, who protected Daphne by turning her into a laurel tree, also called the bay tree. Apollo sadly picked some of the leaves and made himself a crown. Then he promised that the tree would always be evergreen and never wither. In Greece the laurel, or bay tree, is still called Daphne.

Forest and woodland spirits

Every tree can be said to have its roots in the earth, the underworld; its trunk and fruits in the world of humans, where people can reach them; and its branches stretching up to Heaven, carrying the stars.

Forests and woodlands are full of spirits. Deep among the trees, where the light is dim and the forest sounds are strange, it is easy to sense their presence. Trees have been regarded as sacred for a long time. The pillared aisles of old churches are like avenues of tall trees. In ancient Egypt the sycamore tree was sacred; in ancient Rome it was the fig tree, also called the bo tree in India; in Scandinavia it is the ash tree, and in the rest of Europe it is the mighty oak tree.

SATYRS AND FAUNS

The woods are the chosen home of many elves and fairies, and also of some of the nymphs—especially the Dryads and Hamadryads (see pages 32–33). Nymphs are always female, but satyrs and fauns are always male. Called satyrs in Greek mythology and fauns in Roman mythology, they are the lazy, pleasure-loving followers of Pan. Some say that they are the brothers of the nymphs. Others believe that they are the sons of nymphs and goats—which is why they are human down to the waist, aside from their pointed ears and small horns, but have hairy goats' legs and cloven goat's hooves.

Satyrs and fauns are wood genies, who love music and dancing and are usually harmless to humans. Their favorite pastime is chasing nymphs.

34

MISCHIEVOUS LESHIES

The Russian leshies have wild, green hair, long, green beards, and green eyes. Their blood is blue, so their skin has a blue tone. In the winter they hibernate, but in the spring they are at their liveliest and most mischievous. They will let out cries and whistles to confuse travelers and hunters and will lead them around in circles. To escape the spell, humans must take off their clothes and put them on backward and swap their shoes onto the wrong feet.

FINNISH FOREST SPIRITS

The Finnish forest spirits are friendly unless they are annoyed or mistreated. They will lead lost travelers to safety and help hunters find game. When a hunter kills his prey, he must let some of the blood run onto the ground as a gift to the spirit, in gratitude for his help.

Leshies are shape-shifters who can be as tall as trees in the middle of the forest or as tiny as blades of grass at its edge. They cast no shadows.

FOREST AND WOODLAND SPIRITS IN BOOKS AND MOVIES

📖 *Redwall* series
Brian Jacques

📖 *The Lion, the Witch, and the Wardrobe*
C. S. Lewis

📖 *Hexwood*
Diana Wynne Jones

🎥 *FernGully:
The Last Rainforest* (1992)

🎥 *The Wizard of Oz* (1939)

Solitary forest spirits

The solitary forest spirits are among the most vigorous and powerful of them all. The dreaded Bokwus ranges over much of North America. The Green Man—a nature spirit known by many names—can be found throughout northern and eastern Europe. The territory of Herne the Hunter is small—Windsor Great Park in England—but he is no less terrible for that.

Pan likes to appear suddenly, frightening both nymphs and humans. His name is the origin of the word "panic."

PAN

Pan is the son of Hermes, messenger to the Greek gods. He looks like a satyr, with his goats' legs and hooves, his horns, and his beard, but he is not of their kind. He may seem to be part of a group of nymphs and fauns, dancing to the music of his pipes, but really he stands alone—there is only one Pan. He is a rural god found in fields and pastures and woodland glades, caring for shepherds and their flocks and guiding hunters to their prey.

The cult of the horned god Cernunnos was widespread when the Celtic religion flourished in northern Europe. He may still visit a long-lost shrine among the oaks of Windsor Great Park in England.

HERNE THE HUNTER

Close to the site of a fallen oak tree, which once grew in ancient forestland in Windsor, England, the unwary have caught sight of a terrifying figure. He rides a great, black horse, is followed by a pack of phantom hounds, and stag's antlers grow from his head. He is Herne the Hunter, who some say is a Celtic god of the underworld.

Others believe that he was once human, a favorite of a king, until rival hunters persuaded the king to send him away. Herne hanged himself from the oak tree and now haunts the park when the country is in danger.

THE BOKWUS

Native Americans tell stories of the Bokwus—
the dangerous spirit of the spruce tree forests.
Anyone walking alone through the trees can
sense the Bokwus watching and may even
glimpse his war-painted face through the leaves.
He lurks close to the rivers that flow through
the forest and, if he can, drowns fishermen
and travelers so that he can steal their souls.

SOLITARY FOREST SPIRITS IN BOOKS AND MOVIES

- *The Dark is Rising*
  Susan Cooper

- *A Wizard Abroad*
  Diane Duane

- *The Moon of Gomrath*
  Alan Garner

- *The Box of Delights*
  John Masefield

- *Robin of Sherwood—
  Series 1* (1984)

*No matter how often
he is cut down, the Green
Man will always live again.*

THE GREEN MAN

The Green Man is a mysterious
and powerful spirit. No one knows
how ancient he is. He is certainly
preChristian—yet there are carvings
of his leafy head in many Christian
churches. He is the life force of the
plant kingdom, found all over Europe—
sometimes with other names: The Old Man
of the Woods, Jack-in-the-Green, or The Leaf
King. He dies in the winter but is reborn each
spring. Long ago it was believed that human
sacrifice was necessary to ensure his survival.
Even today there are towns in Europe where
his effigy is carried in May Day processions.

Dangerous water spirits

Deep, dark pools are dangerous, and so are rapidly flowing rivers and wide lakes with unexpected currents. These treacherous inland waters tend to have vengeful spirits that are very different from the gentle nymphs and water elementals. The best way to avoid them is to keep far away from the edge.

AHUITZOTL

This vicious creature was the emblem of Ahuitzotl, emperor of the Aztecs from A.D. 1486–1502, and it still bears his name. It is part-dog and part-monkey, and it has a long tail with a monkey hand on the end. It hides in deep water, whimpering to encourage passing humans to come closer. Then it lashes out with its tail, grabs an ankle with its extra hand, and drags its victim underwater to be drowned and then eaten.

This picture of the water spirit Ahuitzotl, lying in wait in a lake, is carved on a stone box that once held the ashes of Emperor Ahuitzotl.

WATER PEOPLE

Among the Slavonic peoples of central and eastern Europe a drowned girl becomes a rusalka—whose sole aim is to drown others. The German nixes are different—they do no harm and sometimes even marry humans. They never cause anyone to drown, but they may dance on the surface of the water if someone is going to drown soon.

The vodyanoi is an eastern European water demon that lurks in millponds, lakes, and streams, waiting to drown humans and animals.

THE BUNYIP

The Australian bunyip haunts rivers, lakes, creeks, swamps, and billabongs. Its name means "devil" in the aboriginal language. It is reported to be a large and ferocious eater of humans, and its bellowing roar can terrify mortals for miles around. It seems to live on the border between reality and fantasy. Many so-called bunyips are probably leopard seals, which certainly are large and noisy. The rest, including those that capture and eat humans, are hostile water spirits, like Ahuitzotl.

DANGEROUS WATER SPIRITS IN BOOKS

📖 *The Kelpie's Pearls*
Molly Hunter

📖 *Silver Moon*
Ian Krykorka

📖 *The Bunyip of Berkeley's Creek*
Jenny Wagner

The water horse can mate with a normal horse. If a foal is born, it will not have magical powers. However, if it is asked to cross a ford, the foal will always lie down in the water.

WATER HORSES

The kelpie of Scotland, the ninnir of Iceland, and the Scandinavian neck are shape-shifters (see page 107) that frequently appear in the form of horses. It is wise to keep far away from them. If a human climbs onto the back of a water horse, it will often plunge into the deepest lake and drown its rider. However if a human gains control of its bridle, the horse can be put to work in the fields. It has the strength of ten land horses, but it does not like to be enslaved and will try every trick in order to escape.

Dangers by the wayside

In the days before travelers were protected within cars, trains, and airplanes, every journey was dangerous and frightening. The roads were narrow, twisted, and unlit, and most people traveled by foot, carrying a flickering lantern to show the way through the night. That was when the stories began—of wandering spirits and phantom lights, of faery dogs, and deadly dangers at crossroads.

THE POOKA

Leading travelers astray is just one of the pastimes of the Little People, but there are some creatures who do nothing else.

The pooka, who may be Robin Goodfellow in disguise (see page 18), is a shaggy horse. He invites the unwary to ride him, then he tips his riders into a lonely bog. However, the pooka is mischievous rather than dangerous.

CROSSROADS

Crossroads are frightening places in many cultures. Some say that any crossing of the ways confuses the flow of earth's energy, creating a psychic whirlpool in which ghosts and spirits may become trapped. Traditionally, executed criminals and witches were taken to crossroads for burial—perhaps to make it difficult for their ghosts to find their way back. The queen of the ghosts, the Greek moon goddess Hecate, is the guardian of crossroads, especially those where three ways meet.

Faery dogs are hunters, around the size of a calf and usually green. The first and second time a faery dog barks it is a warning to flee, but the traveler who hears the third bark is doomed.

PHANTOM LIGHTS

Flickering lights moving across marshy land can sometimes look like slim, elfin figures or like a lantern being carried by an invisible hand. Anyone who follows risks being led into swamps and abandoned when the light vanishes as suddenly as it appeared. In reality it is probably methane gas given off by rotting vegetation that catches light and burns with a pale flame. Alone in the dark, though, it is easier to believe in a mischievous Will O' The Wisp or Jack O'Lantern or in evil spirits and even messengers of death (see pages 124–125).

Phantom lights have other names, including fox fire, *ignis fatuus* (which is Latin for "foolish fire"), and corpse-light, when the lights are seen hovering above a graveyard.

A traveler who trusts a phantom light carried by a goblin or other fairy being is likely to be led into a marsh to drown.

DANGERS BY THE WAYSIDE IN BOOKS AND MOVIES

📖 *The Ghost in the Noonday Sun*
Sid Fleischman

📖 *Jack O'Lantern: A Halloween Tale*
Eric Martone

🎬 *The Nightmare Before Christmas* (1993)

DESERT SPIRITS

Under the surface of the Sahara desert there is a strange world inhabited by a race of spirits who rise up into the world of humans to cause harm. Their spinning dances create sandstorms, and their movements underground cause camels to trip and fall. They will also drink wells dry before thirsty travelers can reach them.

In lonely, rocky places in northern Australia the mimis live in narrow cracks and crevices. They look almost human, but they have such long, thin, fragile bones they are afraid of the wind in case it breaks them. They keep wallabies as pets and eat yams—but they also eat people, so travelers are advised to sing and shout to frighten them off.

The manticore—a savage creature with the body
of a lion, the face of a man, three rows of teeth in each
jaw, the speed of a deer, and a voice like a trumpet—was
almost certainly an exaggerated description of a tiger.

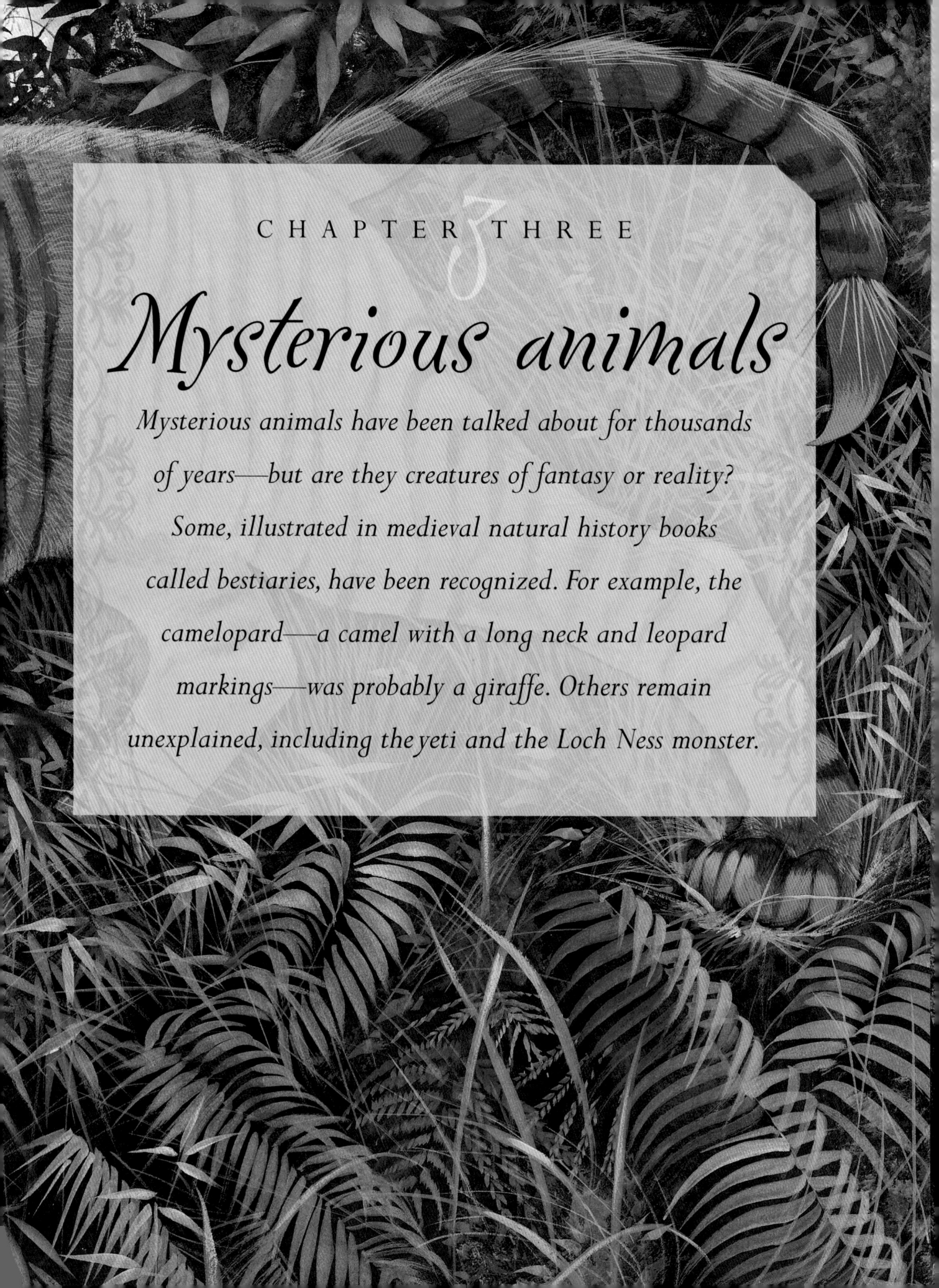

CHAPTER THREE

Mysterious animals

Mysterious animals have been talked about for thousands of years—but are they creatures of fantasy or reality? Some, illustrated in medieval natural history books called bestiaries, have been recognized. For example, the camelopard—a camel with a long neck and leopard markings—was probably a giraffe. Others remain unexplained, including the yeti and the Loch Ness monster.

In lakes

Tales of water monsters come from every country that has large, deep lakes within its borders. These giant lakes are certainly big enough to hide a massive creature, and some are linked to the sea by underground caverns. Reports of sightings go back hundreds of years. Prehistoric rock drawings show animals that were very similar to plesiosaurs and a lot like more recent descriptions of Nessie, Ogopogo, and the rest.

This famous photograph of Nessie, the Loch Ness monster, was taken in 1934 by an English surgeon. In 1994, however, it emerged that the photograph was a fake—the "monster" in the picture is actually a toy submarine rigged up with a plastic neck and head.

LAKE MONSTERS

The Loch Ness monster in Scotland and Ogopogo in Lake Okanogan, Canada, are the most famous lake monsters, but there are many others. A mysterious beast has been reported in Lake Störsjon, Sweden, and a group of monsters was seen in China's Lake Tianchi as recently as 2003. Several have been given nicknames—Issie lurks in Japan's Lake Ikada; Slimy Slim has been seen in Payette Lake, Idaho, U.S. However, most people who have actually seen a lake monster have said that they felt very frightened and overwhelmed.

NESSIE

The Loch Ness monster (nicknamed Nessie) from Loch Ness, Scotland, has been observed on dry land—but only briefly. Once seen, it hurried back to the water, with a rocking motion like a seal on land. Descriptions suggest that it was bigger than any seal though, and its long neck suggested a plesiosaur—an aquatic dinosaur thought to be extinct.

There have been fewer sightings in recent years. Perhaps water pollution and human disturbance have prevented these creatures—whatever they are—from breeding.

OTHER EXPLANATIONS

Sightings of lake monsters could really be glimpses of something else. Deep waters, which are cold at the bottom and warmer at the top, have strong currents that create swirling movements. Floating clumps of rotting vegetation give off gases that can move them through the water on streams of bubbles. Otters or seals could even be mistaken for something strange. Also, no lake monster has been caught—alive or dead—and searches using sonar and divers have found nothing.

However, visibility is bad in the depths, and there have been many reliable witnesses over the years. Also, there are photographs—although some have been revealed to be fakes.

LAKE MONSTERS IN BOOKS AND MOVIES

📖 *Nessie the Loch Ness Monster*
Richard Brassey

📖 *The Water Horse*
Dick King-Smith

📖 *Loch*
Paul Zindel

🎬 *Loch Ness* (1996)

🎬 *Scooby Doo and the Loch Ness Monster* (2004)

The name Ogopogo comes from a British comedy song from the 1920s. The native Canadians are more respectful—they use the name N'haitaka, which means water demon.

In the sea

For hundreds of years people who have sailed the oceans have brought back stories of giant sea serpents. Often they were accused of exaggerating or imagining things. The same disbelief greeted stories of monster waves up to 65 ft. (20m) high. But recently satellite photography has shown that there are freak waves out there, some measuring as high as 100 ft. (30m). So maybe strange creatures really do swim in our oceans and seas.

TWO SIGHTINGS

In l966 John Ridgway and Chay Blyth rowed across the Atlantic Ocean in an open boat, from the U.S. to Ireland. Early one morning, while Blyth slept, Ridgway saw "a writhing shape, two feet [60cm] wide and perhaps 40 feet [12m] long." It swam right toward the boat and then dived and disappeared underneath it.

In 1977 the *Zuiyo Maru*, a Japanese boat fishing off New Zealand, pulled up a huge decomposing body in its trawl nets. It was too heavy and disgusting to keep on board. The crew photographed it, took tissue samples, measured it, and threw it back. In all the years that have followed no one has succeeded in identifying it.

SEA MONSTERS IN BOOKS AND MOVIES

📖 *The Kraken*
Gary Crew

📖 *The Voyage of the Dawn Treader*
C. S. Lewis

📖 *O'Sullivan Stew*
Hudson Talbott

🎥 *20,000 Leagues Under the Sea*
(1954)

🎥 *Godzilla* (1998)

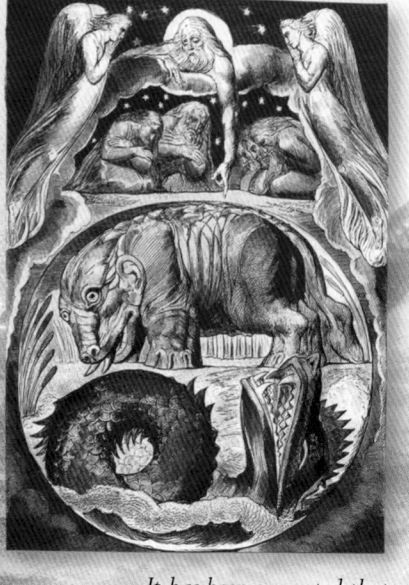

It has been suggested that Leviathan and Behemoth, the huge water monsters from the Old Testament in the Bible, are based on the whale and the hippopotamus. They are larger and more important than that though, as they are not just mythical creatures, but also symbols of divine power.

THE KRAKEN

Most sightings of sea monsters describe serpentine necks and thrashing tails. The legendary kraken is different. Early descriptions claim it to be the size of a small island, with massive tentacles that it uses for swimming and for catching fish. It is not usually aggressive, but it is still dangerous—and even deadly. It is so large that it creates a vast wave when it surfaces, and then it drags the water into a powerful whirlpool when it submerges. Both of these threaten the survival of sailing vessels that are unlucky enough to be closeby. Fishermen, realizing that the water has become unexpectedly shallow beneath their boat, head for shore at once, knowing that they have drifted above a hunting kraken that may rise at any time.

The kraken is now generally thought to be a giant squid or a giant cuttlefish. The giant squid may not be the size of an island, but it can measure up to a monstrous 40 ft. (12m) long, with thrashing tentacles and saucerlike eyes.

The shield bearing the cross of St. George shows that this knight is the saint himself, battling the ancient dragon (see page 54).

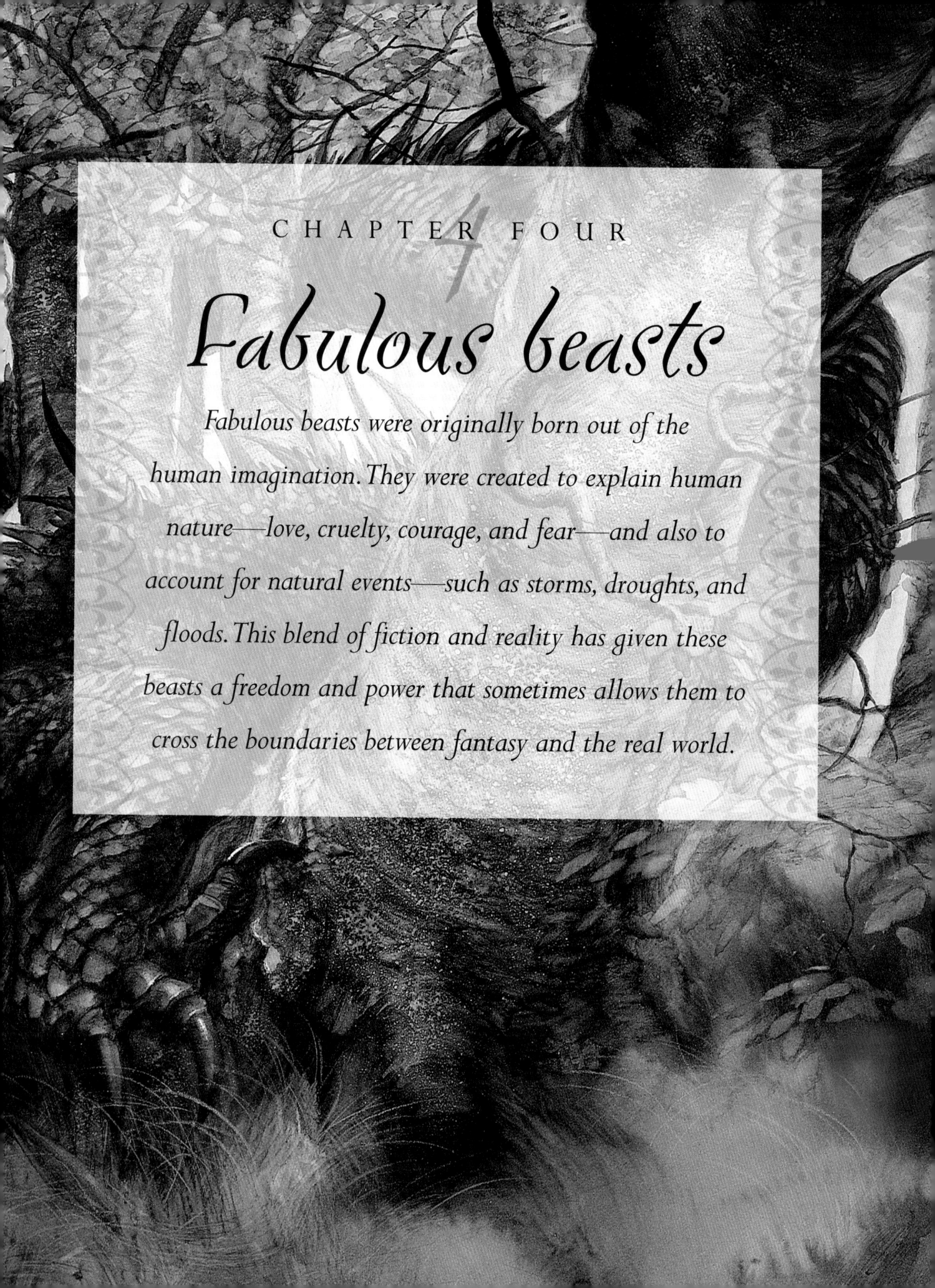

CHAPTER FOUR

Fabulous beasts

Fabulous beasts were originally born out of the human imagination. They were created to explain human nature—love, cruelty, courage, and fear—and also to account for natural events—such as storms, droughts, and floods. This blend of fiction and reality has given these beasts a freedom and power that sometimes allows them to cross the boundaries between fantasy and the real world.

Dragons in the East

Eastern dragons are weather lords, bringers of rain, guardians of springs, rivers, and lakes, and symbols of change. The Japanese dragon is more of a sea or river god. In China the dragons sleep at the bottom of pools during the dry winter season. In the spring they rise up in the form of rain clouds. Storms are caused by dragons fighting in the air and floods by dragons fighting in the water. In the East the dragon is very powerful and usually benevolent.

We know that this dragon is a Chinese imperial dragon because he has five claws. Ordinary Chinese dragons and Korean dragons have four, and Japanese dragons only have three. In ancient China a person could be put to death for using the image of a five-clawed dragon.

BORN FLIERS

Dragons lay eggs that do not hatch for 3,000 years. When their time comes, a hole appears in the shell and a tiny snake emerges. It grows into a full-size dragon in minutes and flies up to the sky in a whirlwind. Unlike Western dragons, Chinese dragons do not have wings. They fly using their own energy.

Dragons are often shown holding or chasing a small globe that may be the moon, or the pearl of wisdom, or the egg that is the source of all life. This globe often has jagged, flamelike shapes coming out of it, which suggests that it could also be a symbol of thunder and lightning.

EASTERN DRAGONS IN STORIES AND MOVIES

📖 *Fire and Wings: Dragon Tales from East and West*
Marianne Carus and Nilesh Mistry

📖 *A Time of Golden Dragons*
Song Nan Zhang

📖 *The Dragon Prince*
Laurence Yep

🎥 *Spirited Away* (2001)

DRAGON LORE

The Yellow Dragon only emerges from his river when a holy man rules the country. It is said that when Fu Hsi, the first of the Ten Emperors, was on the throne, the Yellow Dragon rose up from the water with the earliest Chinese characters marked on his back. In this way he gave the secret of writing to the emperor and so to his people.

In Vietnam carved dragons on roofs are a protection against fire. Dragon fire and earthly fire are opposites. Earthly fire is put out by water. Dragon fire burns in water but is put out by earthly fire.

It was believed that no rain could fall until a dragon rose into the sky, so during times of drought every effort was made to encourage him to wake up and fly. Better still was to disturb two dragons with the hope that they would battle with each other until the storm clouds broke and watered the earth.

53

Dragons in the West

Western dragons are usually dangerous. Some are so evil that they are said to be the devil himself. Like Eastern dragons, they are associated with water, but they are more likely to bring destructive floods than plant-nourishing showers. Unlike Eastern dragons, they are usually hunted and slain.

In the distant past fossilized skulls of dinosaurs or bones of large bears found in caves were thought to be dragon remains. Throughout history there have been hoaxes—including this recent, specially made "baby dragon" preserved in a jar.

DRAGON SLAYERS

St. Michael fought the devil-dragon and threw him out of Heaven, but the most famous dragon slayer is St. George. Legend tells us that in his time (around 2,000 years ago) there was a terrible dragon who lived in a lake and demanded human sacrifices. St. George happened to pass by just as the king's daughter had been tied up and left for the dragon to eat. In some tellings he killed the dragon at once. In others he wounded it, and he and the princess tied it with her sash and led it to the heart of the kingdom to kill it in front of the people.

Dragons are sometimes slain for the hoard of treasure that they guard. Most believe that it is the gold and riches buried with long-dead kings, but some say that it is the gold of the sun, which sets and then rises again, and that the treasure the dragon guards is immortality.

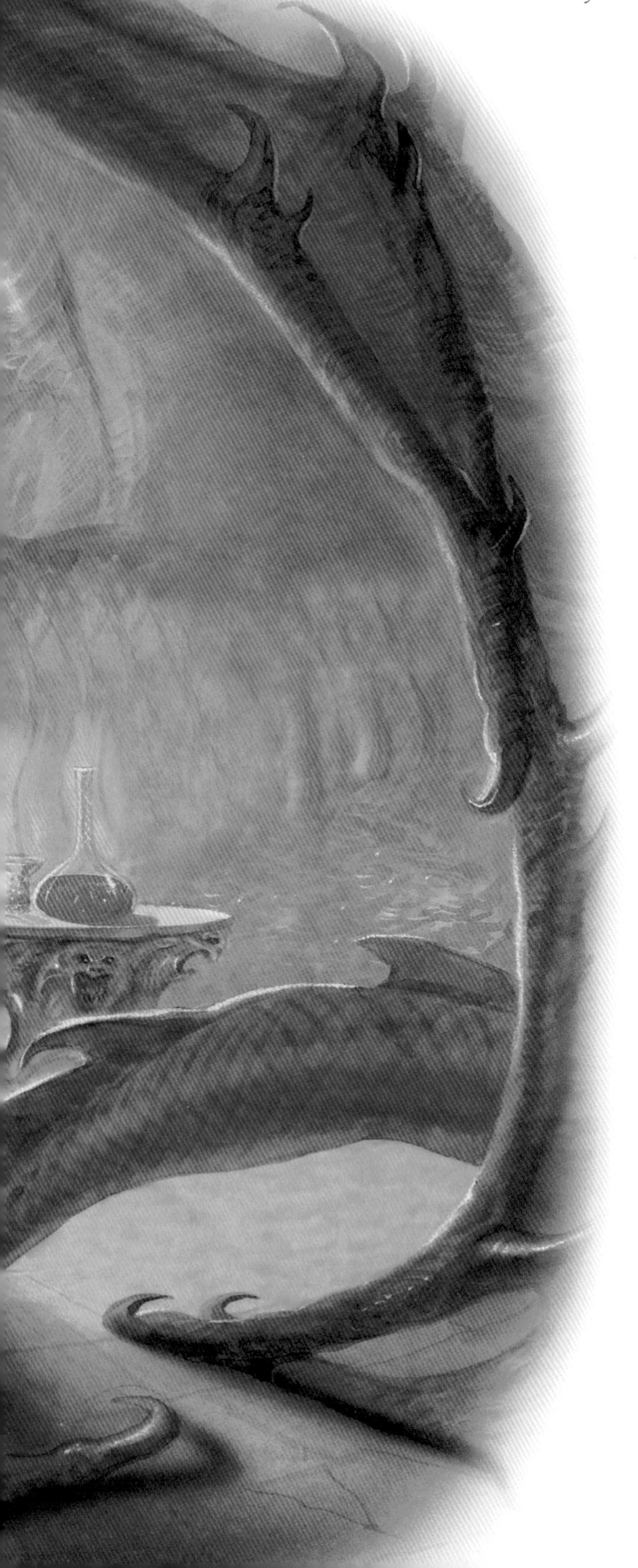

Traditionally the Western dragon is killed with an iron lance. The first iron known to humans is likely to have been found in meteorites. Because meteorites fall to earth from the sky, it was believed that it had come from Heaven and therefore had the power to destroy evil.

GOOD DRAGONS

However, not all Western dragons are bad. When Uther Pendragon (father of King Arthur) was born, two golden dragons appeared in the sky to herald the birth of a chieftain, and dragon images appeared on shields and banners for battles. There are even stories of dragons kept as pets, and also of dragons who help humans such as Falkor the Luck Dragon in *The NeverEnding Story*.

WESTERN DRAGONS IN BOOKS AND MOVIES

📖 *Dr. Ernest Drake's Dragonology*
Ernest Drake

📖 *Eragon*
Christopher Paolini

📖 *The Hobbit*
J. R. R. Tolkien

🎥 *Dragonheart* (1996)

🎥 *The NeverEnding Story* (1984)

Fantasy horses

For hundreds of years horses have been valued more than most other animals. Symbols of power and wealth, horses have been tamed, trained, ridden, sacrificed, buried with kings and warriors, and used to pull peasant carts, royal coaches, and chariots of war. At the same time their speed, strength, beauty, and grace have placed them in the sky with the gods. Mystical, magical horses appear in stories from almost every country on earth.

THE HORSES OF THE SUN

The sun is carried across the sky in a chariot and pulled by a single, powerful stallion or by a team of horses—so we are told by most of the mythologies from the ancient civilizations. In Norse mythology there are two horses—Alsvid the Allswift and Arvak the Early Riser.

The golden chariot of the Greek sun god Helios is drawn by nine white, winged horses, with fire flaring from their nostrils and the light of day pouring from their shining manes.

Many of the other gods traveled behind teams of celestial horses. Odin, the greatest of the Norse gods, is said to have ridden an eight-legged horse, and, as night falls, the moon goddess Selene drives her own pale horse across the heavens.

*Vertebrates (animals with backbones)
have four limbs—either four legs
or two arms and two legs. Pegasus
is one of those rare creatures who,
like winged dragons, have six
limbs—four legs and two wings.*

*Some say that Poseidon (also called Neptune), the god of the sea,
created the first horses. To this day people looking at a stormy
sea refer to the wind-whipped crests of the waves as "white horses."*

PEGASUS

The gentle, winged horse Pegasus sprang from
the blood of the terrible Gorgon Medusa after
Perseus beheaded her. Pegasus flew to the home
of the Muses on Mount Helicon, and to their
delight he created the spring of inspiration,
Hippocrene, by stamping his foot on the ground.

When the hero Bellerophon was given the
task of killing the dreadful Chimera (see page
64), the Greek goddess Athene gave him
a magical golden bridle with which to catch
and tame Pegasus. This meant that he could
fly above the Chimera on the wonderful horse
and rain arrows down on her from a safe
distance. Later he became overambitious
and tried to ride Pegasus to Mount Olympus,
the home of the gods, where no mortal could
go. The gods sent a gadfly to sting and startle
Pegasus, who threw Bellerophon back to earth.
However, the immortal horse was welcomed
into the heavenly stables and has now been
set in the sky as a constellation.

FANTASY HORSES IN BOOKS AND MOVIES

📖 *Stravaganza: City of Stars*
Mary Hoffman

📖 *The Magician's Nephew*
C. S. Lewis

📖 *Pegasus: The Flying Horse*
Jane Yolen

🎬 *Clash of the Titans* (1981)

🎬 *Hercules* (1997)

Fire and feather

*I*magine a creature that has been formed from the lion (King of the Beasts) and the eagle (King of the Birds), large enough to block out the sun, and with the strength to lift a horse and its rider into the sky. Picture a bird that is truly unique, lays no eggs, but is reborn every one thousand years out of its own ashes. Both of these creatures— and the offspring of one—are spoken of in the mountains of India and Arabia.

High up in the Indian mountains, griffins dig gold to make their nests. They also collect the stones known as agate, which have medicinal properties and will protect their chicks from sickness. Humans who try to steal their gold are unlikely to survive—especially as griffins feed their young on human remains. However, adult griffins prefer to eat live horses.

60

THE PHOENIX

The Arabian phoenix is as rare as it is possible to be—there is only one in the whole world. When it knows that it is dying, it builds itself a funeral pyre and sings a beautiful song while the sun sets it alight. Both the pyre and the bird are reduced to ashes. Out of these a new phoenix arises. Traditionally it collects the ashes of its former self and flies, surrounded by other birds, to Heliopolis, the ancient Egyptian City of the Sun. There it delivers the ashes to the priests and flies back to its home in Arabia.

The Feng-Hwang, known as the Chinese phoenix, and the Ho-o, the Japanese phoenix, are somewhat different. Instead of a solitary bird, there is a pair, and their lovely songs are omens of peace and joy.

THE GRIFFIN

Whether its name is spelled griffin or gryphon, this is a majestic beast. It has the body and legs of a lion and the head, wings, and beak of an eagle. Sometimes it has a serpent's tail. Its back is feathered, and its lion's feet are armed with eagle's claws. These claws are prized because, although they cannot purify poison like a unicorn's horn, they can warn of its presence by changing color.

The phoenix is as large as an eagle, and its plumage is dazzlingly beautiful— red, gold, blue, and purple.

THE HIPPOGRIFF

This beast is born when a horse mates with a griffin—something that could never happen because griffins hate horses and eat them when they can. The Roman poet Virgil, who lived between 70 and 19 B.C., referred to crossing griffins with horses as an example of impossibility, and later, in the early 1500s, Ludovico Ariosto created the impossible hippogriff in his epic poem *Orlando Furioso*.

GRIFFINS AND PHOENIXES IN BOOKS AND MOVIES

📖 *The Wrath of Mulgarath*
Tony DiTerlizzi and Holly Black

📖 *The Phoenix and the Carpet*
E. Nesbit

📖 *Year of the Griffin*
Diana Wynne Jones

🎥 *Harry Potter and the Chamber of Secrets* (2002)

Giant birds

Giant birds fly through the folktales, mythology, and fantasy of most countries. The three best known are probably the garuda bird, the roc, and the thunderbird. Giant birds are usually deadly enemies of snakes—except in Central America where the god-king, Quetzalcoatl, is both a bird and a serpent. His name is made up of the words quetzal, a rare Guatemalan bird, and coatl meaning "snake." He is a wind god, the morning and evening star, and the wise ruler who discovered the food, corn.

The very ancient and holy garuda bird is sometimes the chosen steed of the Indian god, Vishnu.

THE GARUDA BIRD

The Indian garuda bird is often shown as part-bird and part-man, although originally he was an eagle. The garuda bird is a demon in Buddhist mythology. In Hindu tales he is the bird of life and the carrier of knowledge, while at the same time he is a creator and a destroyer. In Indonesian mythology he preys on humans. The garuda bird is the enemy of snakes and of the Nagas (see page 67). Even dragons fear him, and his image can scare an Eastern dragon into rising up from his pool and bringing rain.

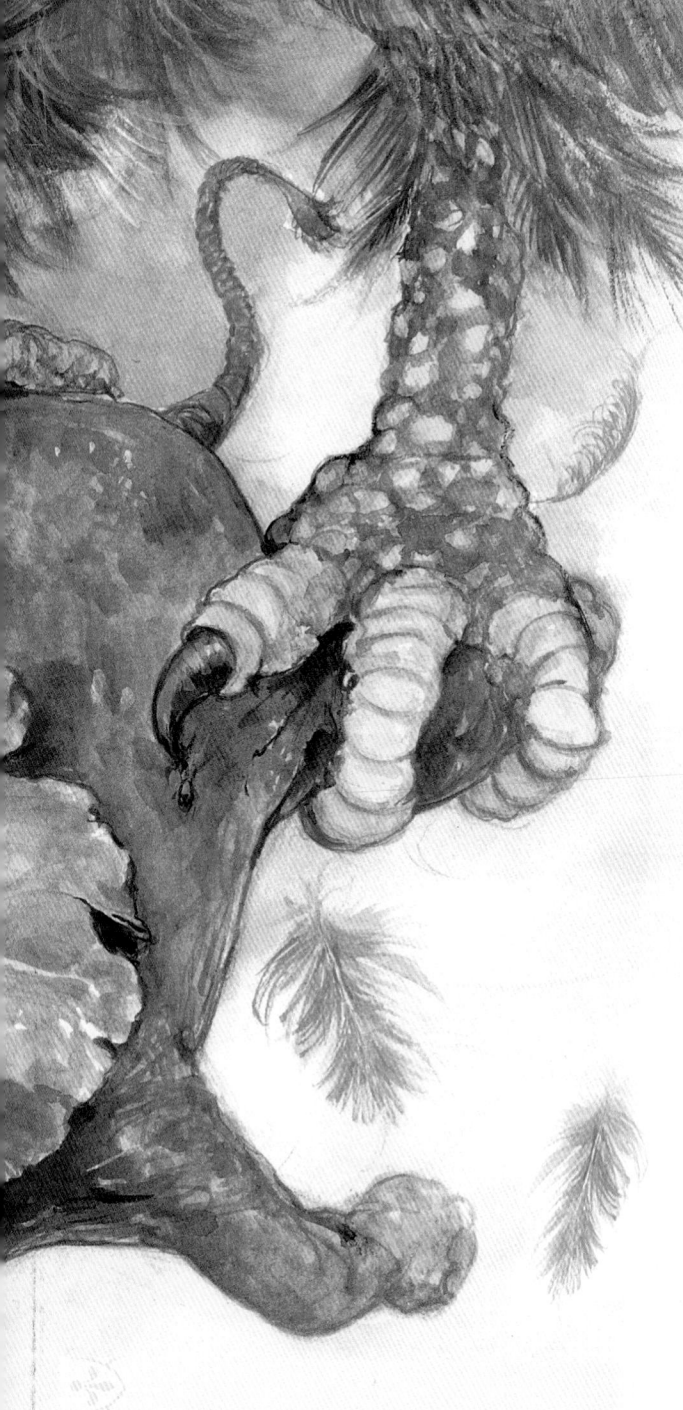

THE ROC

The roc, or rukh (left), is a bird that is so strong, it can lift an elephant as easily as a hawk lifts a mouse. Its wingspan is 50 feet (15m), its egg is taller than a person, and its claws can be made into drinking goblets. Some medieval collectors boasted of owning one of its feathers, but this was probably a frond from the huge raffia palm, also known as the feather palm.

Some descriptions of the roc may be exaggerated accounts of real birds such as the condor of South America. Or they may have been inspired by the sight of an egg from the elephant bird of Madagascar, which became extinct in the 1500s. It was unable to fly, but its egg was enormous.

The thunderbird is a spirit, the symbol of the electrical energy of the storm, which can bring terrible devastation or essential, nurturing rain.

GIANT BIRDS IN BOOKS AND MOVIES

📖 *One Thousand and One Arabian Nights*
Geraldine McCaughrean

📖 *Mythical Birds and Beasts from Many Lands*
Margaret Mayo and Jane Ray

📖 *How Music Came to the World*
Hal Ober

🎥 *The 7th Voyage of Sinbad* (1958)

THUNDERBIRD

Throughout native North American legend the thunderbird represents the storm. His wings make the sound of thunder, his eyes send out lightning flashes, and he brings rain. He is seen in visions rather than in reality because in reality he is surrounded and hidden by dense clouds. The thunderbird may be dangerous, carrying off animals and people, or he may be benevolent, granting good fortune.

Dangerous beasts

Some beasts are so ferocious that not only do they attack with teeth and claws, they can also breathe out fire, poison, or both. They bring destruction to people, other animals, trees, plants, and even to the land itself. The basilisk, or cockatrice, is the worst of these. Not only does it hiss venom into the atmosphere, but a single glance from its glittering eyes means certain death. The Chimera, although fierce, was killed long ago, and even the wyvern is not as dangerous.

THE WYVERN

The wyvern is a flying serpent with two legs, eagle's wings, and a tail that ends in a sharp, arrow-shaped barb. It is sometimes mistaken for a dragon. It is not clear whether or not the wyvern is fire-breathing, but it certainly is aggressive and is known to carry pestilence and plague. When the beast's image is used in heraldry, it is usually as a symbol of strength and fury.

THE CHIMERA

The fire-breathing Chimera (right) was an extraordinary animal with the head and forelegs of a lion, the body of a huge goat, and the tail of a serpent or a dragon. Some say that she had three heads—the lion's at the front, the goat's in the middle of her back, and the reptile's at the rear. Her father was Typhon, spirit of the hurricane, and her mother was Echidna, who was part-woman, part-serpent. After bringing death and devastation for years the Chimera was killed by the Greek hero Bellerophon, riding the winged horse Pegasus.

The cockatrice is so poisonous that if it even drinks from a well, the water will remain polluted for hundreds of years.

BASILISK OR COCKATRICE

This incredibly feared creature takes different forms. The earliest was a small, crowned snake that could kill with its venom or its evil stare. Later medieval travelers said that it was large, with fiery breath and a bellowing roar. The basilisk could be killed if its deadly stare was reflected back at it from a polished surface, or by its archenemy the weasel, or by the crowing of a cockerel. Those who feared meeting it carried a cockerel for protection. Then the description changed again. It was said that the basilisk came from an egg laid by a cockerel and hatched by a toad. It became known as the basilcock and then as the cockatrice. The basilisk is always a snake, but the cockatrice has the head, neck, and legs of a cockerel, a serpentine tail, and sometimes dragon's wings.

DANGEROUS BEASTS IN BOOKS AND MOVIES

📖 *The Cockatrice Boys*
Joan Aiken

📖 *Battle for Castle Cockatrice*
Gerald Durrell

📖 *Pegasus*
Marianna Meyer

🎥 *Harry Potter and the Chamber of Secrets* (2002)

Hydra and the Nagas

Snakes are powerful creatures in fantasy and mythology. Early stories describe a gigantic serpent that encircles the earth, protecting it while also capable of destroying it. Snakes, in their role as water spirits with supernatural powers, have been regarded with awe and fear in almost every country in the world. Some, like the dreadful Hydra, are hostile and cruel. Others, like the mighty Nagas and their wives the Nagini, are wise and, although dangerous, can be friendly. The Hydra is dead and gone—but who knows if the others live on.

THE HYDRA

The Hydra was a massive snake with nine heads on nine separate necks. Its den was in a swamp between a forest and the source of a great river. From there it would emerge to raid the surrounding lands. It fed on cattle, and its poisonous breath destroyed crops, as well as any humans that it encountered.

The Greek hero Heracles (called Hercules in Roman mythology) was given the task of killing it. He and a companion, Iolaus, found its lair. But not only was the Hydra venomous, each time Heracles cut off one of its heads, two more grew in its place. Then Iolaus started a fire in the forest, and with burning branches he sealed each stump after Heracles severed the heads. In this way, the creature was defeated—and Heracles made his arrows deadly by dipping their points in the Hydra's blood.

The Hydra was born from the same parents as the Chimera (see page 64)—Typhon the storm god and Echidna the serpent-woman.

THE NAGAS

The Nagas are snake gods whose kings live in fabulous underwater palaces decorated with pearls and precious stones. They often appear as snakes with many heads, each one hooded like a cobra's. Sometimes they are in human form with a crown of snakes, or human from the waist up and serpent from the waist down. Statues of Nagas are often placed under trees, and the area around the statues is allowed to grow wild as a safe haven for snakes.

Nagas are extremely powerful, and the only creature they fear is the gigantic Garuda Bird. They are moody, dangerous if made angry, but generous if they are treated with respect. Nagas are also water lords who have a lot in common with dragons—controlling rain clouds, protecting pools, lakes, and rivers, and also guarding treasures. Despite this, they can marry mortals, and some ancient families in India are said to be descended from them.

Here the Buddha is seated on the coils of a Naga who, calmed by his gentle teachings, shelters him with its hooded heads.

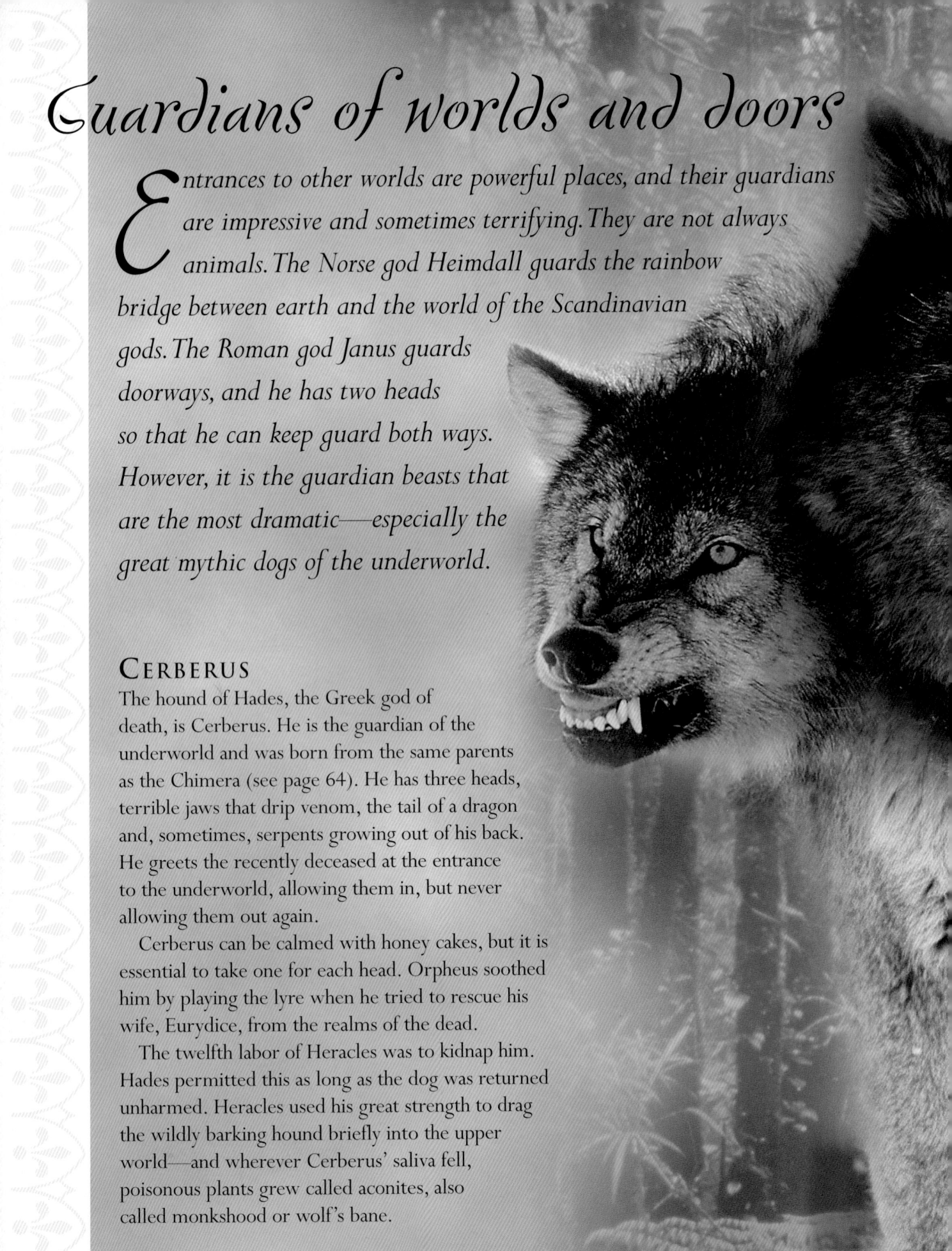

Guardians of worlds and doors

Entrances to other worlds are powerful places, and their guardians are impressive and sometimes terrifying. They are not always animals. The Norse god Heimdall guards the rainbow bridge between earth and the world of the Scandinavian gods. The Roman god Janus guards doorways, and he has two heads so that he can keep guard both ways. However, it is the guardian beasts that are the most dramatic—especially the great mythic dogs of the underworld.

CERBERUS

The hound of Hades, the Greek god of death, is Cerberus. He is the guardian of the underworld and was born from the same parents as the Chimera (see page 64). He has three heads, terrible jaws that drip venom, the tail of a dragon and, sometimes, serpents growing out of his back. He greets the recently deceased at the entrance to the underworld, allowing them in, but never allowing them out again.

Cerberus can be calmed with honey cakes, but it is essential to take one for each head. Orpheus soothed him by playing the lyre when he tried to rescue his wife, Eurydice, from the realms of the dead.

The twelfth labor of Heracles was to kidnap him. Hades permitted this as long as the dog was returned unharmed. Heracles used his great strength to drag the wildly barking hound briefly into the upper world—and wherever Cerberus' saliva fell, poisonous plants grew called aconites, also called monkshood or wolf's bane.

*Cerberus is the huge and terrible
guardian dog of the underworld.
His name comes from the Greek
word* kerberos, *meaning
"demon of the pit."*

GUARDIAN BEASTS IN BOOKS AND MOVIES

📖 *Prince Orpheus*
Paule Du Bouchet

📖 *Tales of the Norse Gods*
Barbara Leonie Picard

📖 *The Twelve Labors of Hercules*
James Riordan

🎥 *Harry Potter and the
Sorcerer's Stone* (2001)

*Janus, the Roman
god of gates, doors,
and passageways,
is also the god of
new beginnings.
The month
of January is
named after him.*

GARM AND THE DOGS OF YAMA

In Norse mythology Hel is the goddess
of Helheim, the Land of the Dead, and Garm
is her hound, the guardian of death's gate. He
is an enormous creature with four eyes. His
body is usually covered in the blood of the slain.

In Indian teachings Yama was the first being
to die, and so he reigns in the next world and
guides those who must journey to it. His
kingdom is not the dark underworld, but the
bright outer sky. Yama's four-eyed hounds—
Syama the Black and Sabala the Spotted—are
as fierce as Cerberus or Garm, but they are also
helpful. They are often sent out to find the dead
and lead them safely to Yama's kingdom of light.
Even so, the dead are given raw meat for their
journey in order to pacify the hounds.

There are nine Muses. They are
generally agreed to be Clio for history; Calliope
for epic poetry; Erato for love poetry; Euterpe for music;
Thalia for comedy; Melpomene for tragedy; Terpsichore
for dance; Polyhymnia for hymns; and Urania for astronomy.

CHAPTER FIVE

Mythical beings

Some mythical beings, such as Sirens, centaurs, and Cyclops, are the creations of classical mythology. Others, such as mermaids and giants, owe their existence partially to travelers' tales. However, they have all found their way in one form or another into the world of fantasy. In any case, it could be said that all ideas—including fantastical ones—come from those early Greek mythical beings, the classical Muses, the goddesses of inspiration.

Beautiful but dangerous

In ancient Greece and Rome boats were propelled by oarsmen, whose work was especially difficult if the currents and tides were against them. Without maps or charts, they relied on the words of others to guide them. Having no instruments of navigation, they stayed close to land, risking shallows and hidden rocks. Sea travel was perilous, and the ever-present dangers were given many names such as Scylla, Charybdis, and the legendary Sirens.

The hero Odysseus, or Ulysses, was saved from the Sirens by the enchantress Circe. Following her advice, he ordered his men to melt wax to block their ears. Then Odysseus asked to be tied to the ship's mast so that he could hear the Sirens' songs but would not be able to change the direction of the ship, however persuasive they were.

THE SIRENS

The Sirens had the bodies and feet of birds, but they had the faces and upper bodies of beautiful women. They lived on a small, barren island off southern Italy. They were famous for the beauty of their singing voices and for their songs, which offered knowledge of the past and the future to all who heard them. Despite this, they were deadly. Mariners, lured to the island by their singing, found the Sirens surrounded by the bones and corpses of their earlier victims and knew that they were trapped.

Later Jason and the Argonauts sailed by in their quest for the Golden Fleece. Orpheus, son of the god Apollo, was with them, and he played the lyre and sang even more beautifully than the Sirens. His songs overcame them, and the Sirens were turned into rocks for eternity.

SCYLLA AND CHARYBDIS

Scylla once was a water nymph, and there are many different stories about how she became a monster. In all of them, however, it was a jealous goddess or enchantress who changed her into a writhing, serpentlike form with six heads and a voice like the howling of dogs. She lived in a cave, probably in the Straits of Medina between Italy and Sicily, and sent out her heads on their long, snakelike necks to snatch sailors from their ships and devour them.

Across from her—on the other side of the narrow straits— was Charybdis (left), a powerful whirlpool strong enough to swallow the largest vessel. Navigating between these two terrors was a matter of life and death.

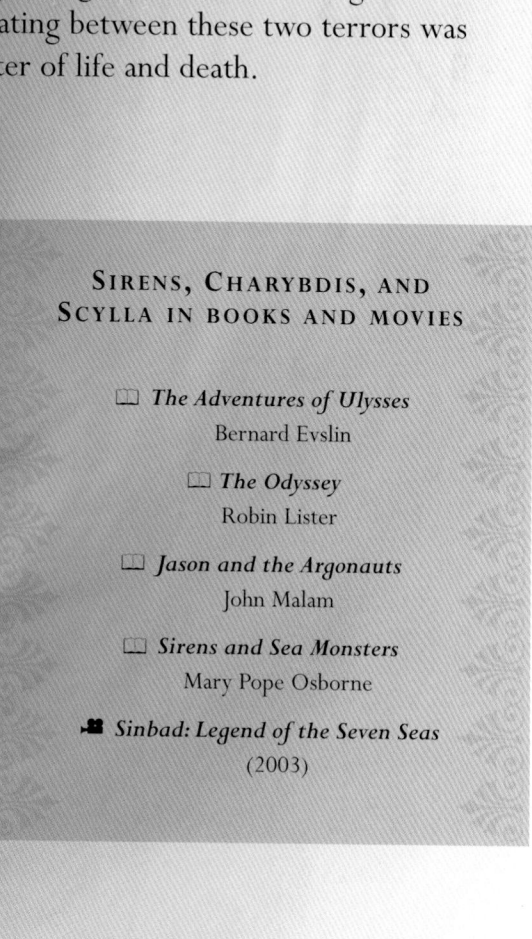

SIRENS, CHARYBDIS, AND SCYLLA IN BOOKS AND MOVIES

📖 *The Adventures of Ulysses*
Bernard Evslin

📖 *The Odyssey*
Robin Lister

📖 *Jason and the Argonauts*
John Malam

📖 *Sirens and Sea Monsters*
Mary Pope Osborne

🎥 *Sinbad: Legend of the Seven Seas*
(2003)

Hideous and dangerous

The Furies, the Gorgons, and the Harpies are among the most ferocious and hideous characters in Greek mythology. On rare occasions the Furies can deliver good fortune, but most of the time they, like the others, bring terror.

THE GORGONS

The three Gorgon—also known as The Grim Ones—are Euryale the Wanderer, Sthenno the Strong One, and Medusa the Ruler. Sometimes they have the heads of women, sometimes of dogs or lions, and sometimes they have tusks like a wild boar. One glance from a Gorgon can turn a person into stone. Two of the dreaded sisters are immortal, but Medusa was mortal. Perseus succeeded in killing Medusa by using her reflection in his shield to guide his hand and then cutting off her head. When drops of her blood fell into the sea, they became scarlet coral branches—these are still known as Gorgonia today.

THE FURIES

It is never wise to speak the name of the Furies. Instead call them "the Kindly Ones" in order to calm them. There are three—Alecto the Endless, Tisiphone the Punisher, and Megaera the Jealous Rager. The furies are fearsome crones, with the heads of dogs and hair made of snakes. They carry torches to hunt down wrongdoers and whips with metal studs to deliver vicious beatings.

The Furies are avengers—avenging anyone who has been harmed by lies or, worse, murdered by their children.

THE HARPIES

No one knows how many Harpies there are, but they are also called "the Seizers" or "the Snatchers" because they carry away human beings or steal their food. Some say that they were once beautiful—and they certainly have the faces and breasts of women, but they have the bodies and wings of vultures and terrible, long claws. They are among the most dangerous creatures of the underworld, appearing in storms and whirlwinds and leaving behind a foul and putrid stench.

The only thing that frightens Harpies away is the sound made by a brazen (brass) instrument.

All the Gorgons, including Medusa—the best-known—have writhing serpents instead of hair.

GORGONS, FURIES, AND HARPIES IN BOOKS AND MOVIES

📖 *The Odyssey*
Homer

📖 *Perseus*
Geraldine McCaughrean

🎬 *Clash of the Titans* (1981)

🎬 *The 7th Voyage of Sinbad* (1958)

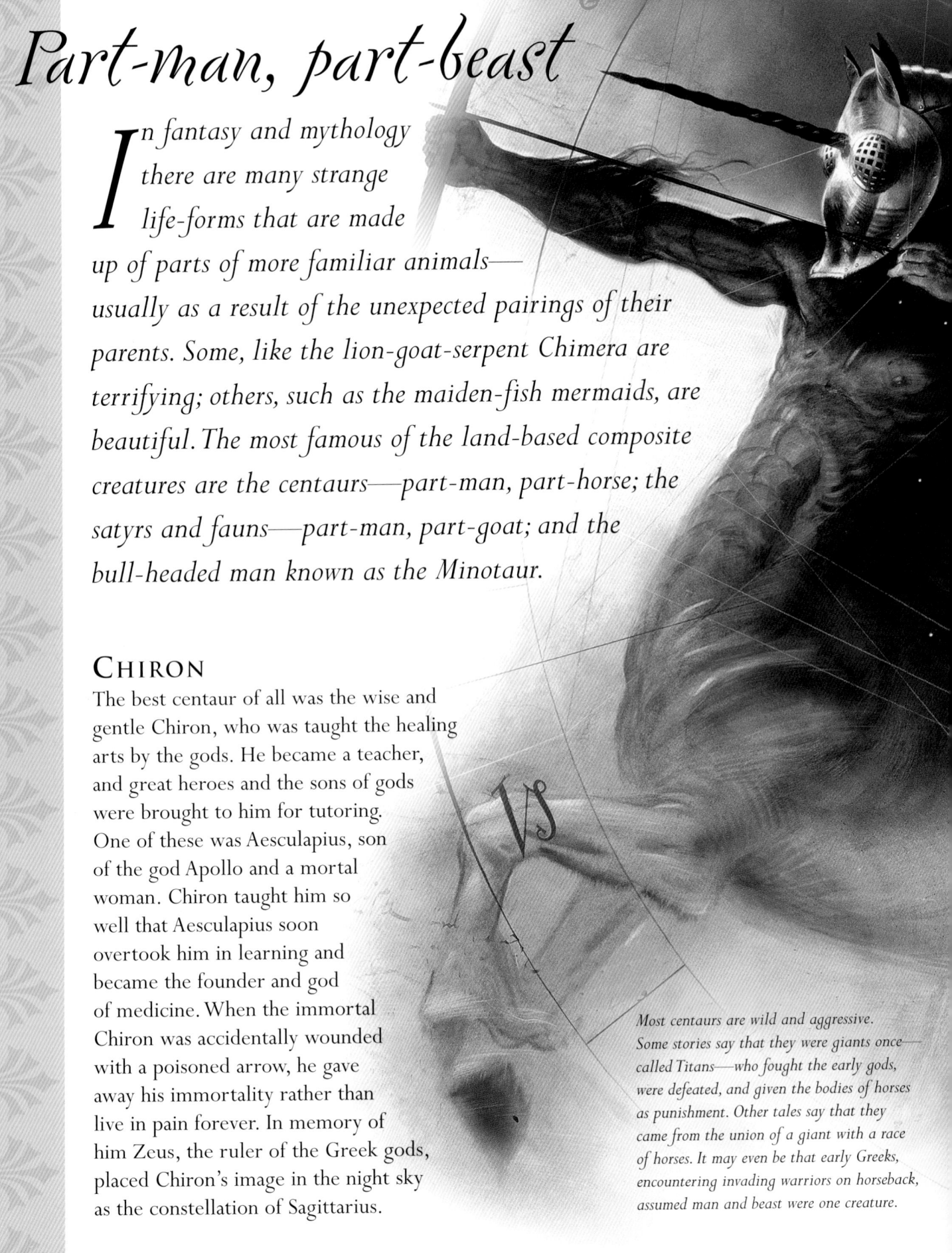

Part-man, part-beast

In fantasy and mythology there are many strange life-forms that are made up of parts of more familiar animals— usually as a result of the unexpected pairings of their parents. Some, like the lion-goat-serpent Chimera are terrifying; others, such as the maiden-fish mermaids, are beautiful. The most famous of the land-based composite creatures are the centaurs—part-man, part-horse; the satyrs and fauns—part-man, part-goat; and the bull-headed man known as the Minotaur.

CHIRON

The best centaur of all was the wise and gentle Chiron, who was taught the healing arts by the gods. He became a teacher, and great heroes and the sons of gods were brought to him for tutoring. One of these was Aesculapius, son of the god Apollo and a mortal woman. Chiron taught him so well that Aesculapius soon overtook him in learning and became the founder and god of medicine. When the immortal Chiron was accidentally wounded with a poisoned arrow, he gave away his immortality rather than live in pain forever. In memory of him Zeus, the ruler of the Greek gods, placed Chiron's image in the night sky as the constellation of Sagittarius.

Most centaurs are wild and aggressive. Some stories say that they were giants once— called Titans—who fought the early gods, were defeated, and given the bodies of horses as punishment. Other tales say that they came from the union of a giant with a race of horses. It may even be that early Greeks, encountering invading warriors on horseback, assumed man and beast were one creature.

It is possible that the story of the Minotaur originated in early Minoan religious ceremonies in which a sacred bull was sacrificed in the center of a symbolic maze.

15th-century zodiac sign for Sagittarius.

THE MINOTAUR

The Minotaur no longer exists. The father of this savage monster was a beautiful bull, and his mother was the wife of King Minos of Crete. When the bull-headed monster was born to his queen, King Minos had an intricate labyrinth built to contain the beast. Later after Aigeus, King of Athens, caused the death of Minos' son, Minos made war on Athens and defeated it. He forced Aigeus to send him a tribute of seven maidens and seven young men every nine years. These fourteen youths were driven into the immense labyrinth. Unable to find their way out, they were doomed to meet the dreadful Minotaur, who devoured them. At last the hero Theseus, intent on killing the creature, chose to be among the victims. Fortunately King Minos' daughter Ariadne fell in love with him and gave him a ball of thread, telling him to tie one end at the opening of the labyrinth and unravel it as he went. Theseus succeeded in killing the Minotaur with his bare hands and then followed the thread out of the maze to safety.

CENTAURS AND THE MINOTAUR IN BOOKS AND MOVIES

📖 *Shadow of the Minotaur*
Alan Gibbons

📖 *The Horse and His Boy*
C. S. Lewis

📖 *Jason and the Gorgon's Blood*
Jane Yolen

🎥 *Fantasia* (1940)

🎥 *The Lion, the Witch, and the Wardrobe* (2005)

Riddles and prophecies

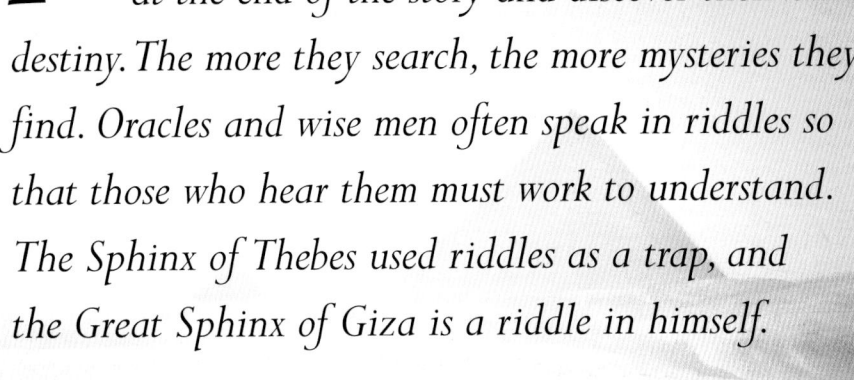

For thousands of years people have wanted to understand the world—as well as to look at the end of the story and discover their own destiny. The more they search, the more mysteries they find. Oracles and wise men often speak in riddles so that those who hear them must work to understand. The Sphinx of Thebes used riddles as a trap, and the Great Sphinx of Giza is a riddle in himself.

The Delphic oracle's mysterious words were translated by priests —and sometimes misunderstood. When King Croesus (died c. 546 B.C.) asked if he should invade Persia (modern-day Iran), she said that if he did, a mighty empire would fall. Expecting victory, he invaded—but it was his own empire that was destroyed.

ORACLES

An oracle has the ability to see into the future and speak words of wisdom to those who seek information.

The oracle at Delphi, Greece, is one of the most famous. Here, within the temple of Apollo, the Greek god of prophecy, was a narrow opening through which vapors rose from deep within the earth. Inside, on a tripod above the fissure, sat the oracle herself in a trance. She was consulted by kings and warriors, who gave great wealth to the shrine.

Crystal balls—globes of quartz crystal as clear as glass—have been believed to have magical properties for a long time. Traditionally a crystal ball is used for seeing the future. Some claim to see images of what is to come in the glass; others say that gazing into the crystal focuses the psychic powers, and that the visions the fortune-teller sees are actually in the mind.

THE GREAT SPHINX OF GIZA

The Great Sphinx still keeps his secrets. No one can be certain who made him or when—although it was at least 4,500 years ago. He is carved out of limestone bedrock, with a lion's body and a man's head. Other Egyptian sphinxes are set in pairs or rows, guarding temples and tombs, but the Great Sphinx stands alone close to the great Pyramid of Khafre. According to the inscription on the stone slab between his paws, he appeared in a dream to Thutmose IV (b. 1425 B.C.) when he was still a prince, asking him to clear the sand in exchange for the kingship of Egypt. Thutmose obeyed and the sphinx kept his part of the bargain.

THE SPHINX OF THEBES

The ancient city of Thebes in Upper Egypt was at one time stalked by a monstrous sphinx with the body of a lion, the head of a woman, and huge wings. She asked riddles of passing travelers— and when they gave her the wrong answer, she devoured them. At last a man named Oedipus approached, and she gave him this riddle: "What goes on four feet, on two feet and three, but the more feet it goes on the weaker it be?" Oedipus gave the correct answer: "A man—he crawls on all fours as a baby, walks on two feet as an adult, and uses a walking stick in old age." The sphinx killed herself in a fury, and Oedipus was crowned king of Thebes.

The Great Sphinx of Giza has been badly damaged over time by weather and frequently buried deep in drifting sand. The sacred cobra on his forehead shows that he is royal.

RIDDLES AND PROPHECIES IN BOOKS AND MOVIES

📖 *The Oracle Betrayed*
Catherine Fisher

📖 *Northern Lights*
Philip Pullman

📖 *The Hobbit*
J. R. R. Tolkien

🎬 *The Dark Crystal* (1982)

Giants in the land

In British folklore Gog and Magog are two giants who protect the city of London and whose likenesses have been carried in the annual Lord Mayor's procession since the reign of King Henry V (1387–1422).

*I*n the creation myths of many civilizations giants are the earliest beings. They are the massive forces of chaos and nature. Sometimes they built the mountains; sometimes their bodies formed the mountains. In ancient Greece the Titans were the giant children of Gaea the Earth and Uranus the Sky. When the gods were born, the Titans fought with them but were defeated.

ATLAS

Atlas was the leader of the Titans and possibly the king of the legendary land of Atlantis. During the great war between the gods and the Titans Atlas stormed the gods' stronghold of Mount Olympus. When the gods eventually triumphed, the Titans were banished— all except Atlas who was sentenced to carry the skies on his shoulders for all eternity. When Perseus flew past him carrying the head of the Gorgon Medusa, Atlas was turned into stone. He is now the Atlas Mountains, in northwest Africa.

Atlas is usually shown supporting the earth instead of the skies. In 1595 the Flemish mapmaker Mercator produced the first modern collection of maps of the world, with a picture of Atlas at the front—and that is how books of maps came to be called atlases.

SHAPING THE LANDSCAPE

The huge Asilky of Russia piled up the mountains and scooped out riverbeds and lakes, but like the Titans, they threatened the gods and were destroyed. The frost giants of Scandinavia carved out valleys and mountain ranges, and their melting bodies formed rivers. Many of the giants fought, hurling enormous stones at each other. This can explain ancient upright stones, sometimes standing in rows or in circles, and also huge rocks lying many miles from where they were formed. However, there are other explanations—that prehistoric people put up the standing stones and that glaciers carried the rocks across the landscape during the Ice Age.

GIANT KILLERS

Fairy-tale giants are huge and strong, but they are also stupid and easily outwitted. Jack the Giant Killer defeated one with a simple trick. He challenged the giant to an eating contest, concealing a bag under his clothes. As the giant ate, Jack slipped his own food into the bag. As the giant's stomach filled and swelled, Jack's stomach appeared to swell as well. At last, saying that he needed to make more space, Jack plunged his knife into the bag and let food spill out. The giant seized his own knife and copied Jack's action—and killed himself.

GIANTS IN BOOKS AND MOVIES

📖 *The BFG*
Roald Dahl

📖 *The Selfish Giant*
Oscar Wilde

🎬 *Harry Potter and the Chamber of Secrets* (2002)

🎬 *The Iron Giant* (1999)

🎬 *Jack and the Beanstalk: The Real Story* (2001)

🎬 *The Princess Bride* (1987)

Ogres and trolls

Giants may either be good or bad, but ogres are always bad and dangerous. It is thought that the word "ogre" was first used by Charles Perrault in his collection of fairy tales published in France in A.D. 1697. An English translation was published in the early 1700s under the title Mother Goose Tales. Scandinavian trolls are also extremely dangerous, and like ogres, they enjoy eating human flesh.

THE CYCLOPS

The first group of one-eyed giants called Cyclops were, like the Titans, the children of Gaea and Uranus. The Cyclops were blacksmiths who forged the thunderbolts for the great god Zeus (the Roman god Jupiter) and the trident of Poseidon (the Roman god Neptune). Their forges burned in the hearts of volcanoes, and the sound of their hammering shook the earth. Their human brides gave birth to the second group of giants, who lived as shepherds, herding flocks of giant sheep. A Cyclops imprisoned the ancient Greek hero Odysseus, along with all Odysseus' men, in his cavern. The Cyclops ate some of them and promised to devour the rest of them later. To escape, Odysseus used a sharpened stake to blind the Cyclops while he slept. When the enraged giant drove his sheep out to graze, he checked that his prisoners were not riding them to freedom—but he did not guess that they were clinging to the wool on the sheep's undersides.

TROLLS

The trolls from Scandinavian myths (right) are enormous creatures, hideously ugly, extremely strong, and thoroughly evil-minded. They live in caves, hiding deep inside during the day and lumbering out at night to hunt. Their prey includes humans. The best defense is to run fast enough to lure them far away from their underground homes so that they are outside when the sun rises—because exposure to sunlight turns them into stone. The trows of the British Shetland Islands are similar creatures, whose ancestors arrived with the Viking invaders.

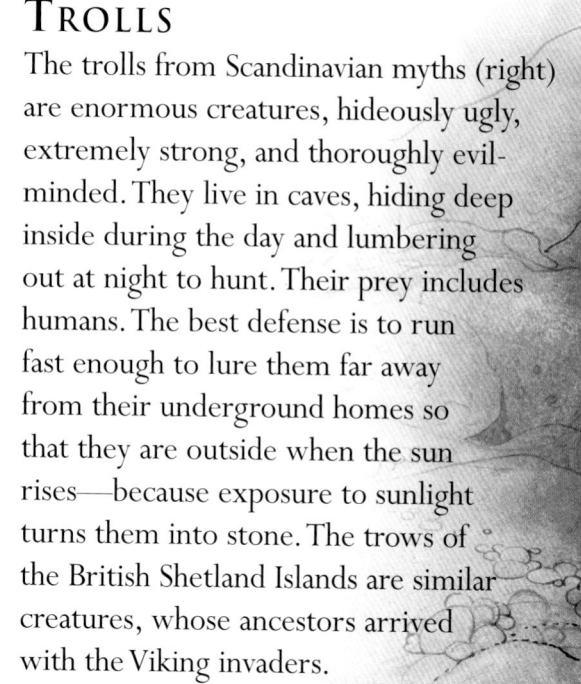

Elephant skulls, with the single enormous nose hole behind the trunk, could be mistaken for the skulls of one-eyed giants. Skulls of early types of elephants have been found in several countries, including Greece, and could be the origin of the story of the Cyclops.

OGRES AND TROLLS IN BOOKS AND MOVIES

📖 *Sea of Trolls*
Nancy Farmer

📖 *Troll Fell*
Katherine Langrish

📖 *The Hobbit*
J. R. R. Tolkien

🎥 *The Goonies* (1985)

🎥 *Shrek* (2001)

THE WINDIGO

The Windigo is a Native American ogrelike creature, who is also a shape-shifter. He is an evil spirit who roams the forests and wilderness of southern Canada in search of human meat. The Windigo can take the form of a giant gray wolf, but often he is seen as a man, tall as a mighty tree, who travels in blizzards so that he cannot easily be seen. He has great strength and speed and can let out a scream so terrifying that his victim is paralyzed with fear and unable to run. He has something in common with a werewolf, because anyone who is bitten but escapes will inevitably become a Windigo.

Sea beings

Our distant ancestors came from the sea, and the memory remains in our salty blood and tears. It has such a hold on us—and is so vast and mysterious—that it is easy to believe it is as much the home of the gods as the shifting sky or the shadowy underworld. Every civilization had its sea gods, riding the waves and raising or calming storms. Perhaps the greatest of these is Poseidon.

The word "trident" means three-toothed. It is a three-pronged staff used by fishermen in Greece and wielded by the sea god known as Poseidon, or Neptune. In the Christian belief it is carried by the devil and used to torment sinners.

POSEIDON (NEPTUNE)

The powerful Greek god Poseidon is also known as Neptune in Roman mythology. He rules the sea from his palace of coral and gemstones, just as Zeus rules the sky from Mount Olympus and Hades governs the underworld. The earth is shared between the three. Poseidon has the power to create earthquakes, storms, and shipwrecks by striking the ground with his trident. If he is in a good mood though, he will calm the seas, which is why sailors try not to ever offend him.

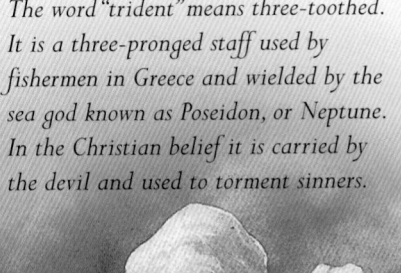

The hippocampus is part-dolphin and part-horse. It is a massive creature that draws the chariot of Poseidon, but the name is also given to the tiny, delicate pipefish known as a sea horse.

The conch is a sea creature whose shell can become a type of bugle when the animal is removed and the tip is broken away to form a mouthpiece. The Hindu god Vishnu used a conch, and it is still used in Hindu religious ceremonies, including weddings. The Triton conch, the largest of its type, can reach up to 16 in. (40cm) in length.

SEA BEINGS IN BOOKS AND MOVIES

📖 *The Sea Fairies*
L. Frank Baum

📖 *Harry Potter and the Goblet of Fire*
J. K. Rowling

📖 *Nicholas Pipe*
Robert D. San Souci

📖 *The Missing Link*
Kate Thompson

🎬 *The Little Mermaid*
(1989)

TRITON AND THE TRITONS

The first Triton was the son of Poseidon and Amphitrite, one of the Nereids. Half-man and half-fish, his fish tail is forked, and his body is covered in scales. He uses the largest of the conch shells—known as the Tritons' trumpet—as a horn. There are many other Tritons, both male and female. All blow on conch shells and have forked fish tails, and some—the centauro-tritons—also have the front legs of horses. They are wild and noisy and escort the chariots of the sea gods. In the sky the largest moon of the planet Neptune has been named Triton.

THE HALFWAY PEOPLE

The First Nation tribes of Canada, who spend much of the summer fishing in the sea, are just one of many groups with stories of the halfway people, half-men and half-fish, who raise storms if they are angered. Japan has the Ningyo—not a human with a fish tail, but a fish with a human head—and descriptions of the ugly Margyr of Greenland make it sound like a walrus. It seems likely that a number of reported sightings have been of other species—walrus, seal, dugong, and manatee—all of which will raise their heads out of the water to stare at passing boats. Certainly many reports suggest that mermen and merwomen are not older relatives of mermaids, but creatures of a different race.

Mermaids

In the days when sea vessels were powered by oarsmen or by the wind in their sails, mermaids were occasionally described as unusual looking, with animal heads instead of than human heads. They have grown more beautiful over time and are now as pretty as nymphs with fish tails. Like the Sirens, they have wonderful singing voices, and like the seal women, they share the possibility of bearing children to mortal men.

THE LORE OF MERMAIDS

The image of a lovely fish-tailed woman, sitting on a rock gazing into a mirror and combing her long hair, is familiar, and her story starts at least as far back as ancient Babylon.

The mermaid is sometimes said to have been the fantasy of men who had been out at sea for too long in a time when a voyage could last for years. Yet a group of divers off the coast of Hawaii saw a mermaid as recently as 1998. Or perhaps the mermaid is actually a Siren (see page 72), carrying not a mirror but a lyre (the ancient stringed instrument of the Sirens) and not a comb but a plectrum to pluck its strings.

Perhaps the mermaid is as real as a dolphin. Or maybe she is a spirit of the sea and as beautiful and dangerous as the ocean she lives in.

This fake mermaid is from Aden, Yemen. Such deceptions are known as "Jenny Hanivers"—although no one is sure where the name originated from. The fake creatures are made from parts of other animals.

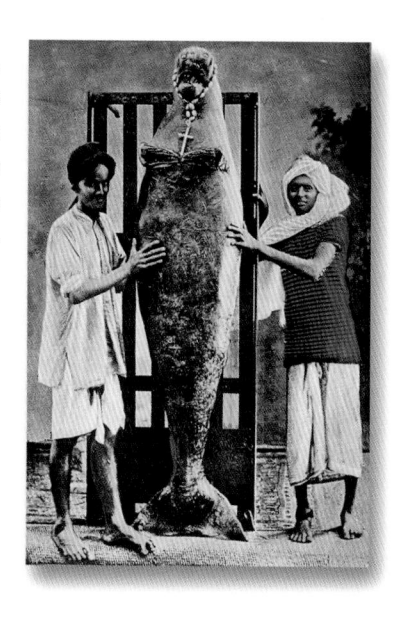

It has always been believed that mermaids can foretell the future, so perhaps they sing not to lure ships onto rocks, but to warn of a coming storm.

SEAL WOMEN

Seal women—called selkies in the British Orkney Islands—are known in remote areas where seals come ashore to give birth to their pups. It is said that every ninth night the seals take off their skins and become humans. They prefer not to be seen, but it has happened more than once that a man secretly watching has fallen in love with a seal woman. In each case he has stolen and hidden her sealskin, forcing her to remain in human form after which he marries her and has children and a happy life with her. In each case the seal woman has eventually found her sealskin, put it on, and slipped back into the sea never to be seen again. There are still families today whose ancestors claim descent from such a marriage.

MERMAIDS IN BOOKS AND MOVIES

📖 *The Litle Mermaid*
Hans Christian Andersen

📖 *Half-Human*
Bruce Coville

📖 *Wet Magic*
E. Nesbit

🎥 *The Secret of Roan Inish* (1994)

🎥 *Splash* (1984)

CHAPTER SIX

Magic and spells

Magic is an ancient art practiced by wizards, witches, sorcerers, and their kind. These powerful people can use their knowledge for good or for evil. They may work with many devices, including spells. These can be a single word or several, often chanted as part of a ritual, and used in different ways—to protect or damage; to alter or make invisible; to see or change the future.

Witches and wise women

Witches—perhaps surprisingly—can be either male or female. There are evil witches who follow the devil and wish harm on others, and there are good witches who are followers of the pagan religion Wicca—the Old English word for "witch." Wise women are knowledgeable about natural forces and living things—their skills could seem almost supernatural. The witches of fantasy can behave like any or all of these.

WARLOCKS

A dangerous male witch is called a warlock. The word comes from the Old English word *war loga*, meaning "liar" or "deceiver," and is used for someone who has sold their soul to the great liar and deceiver, the devil. Male witches who are only interested in healing, rainmaking, and encouraging plants to grow and animals to thrive are not warlocks.

WICCA

Modern Wicca began in the late 1930s, but its followers engage in the beliefs of the ancient Egyptians and the early Celts. They believe in an earth goddess and the horned god, Cernunnos— sometimes called Herne the Hunter (see page 36)—who has no connection with the devil. Wiccans believe that whatever a person does comes back to them three times as strong. Therefore, all Wiccan magic is intended to do good, because a harmful spell would certainly backfire.

WITCHES AND WISE WOMEN IN BOOKS AND MOVIES

📖 *The Spook's Apprentice*
Joseph Delaney

📖 *The Worst Witch*
Jill Murphy

📖 *The Wee Free Men*
Terry Pratchett

🎥 *Hocus Pocus* (1993)

🎥 *Willow* (1988)

🎥 *The Witches* (1990)

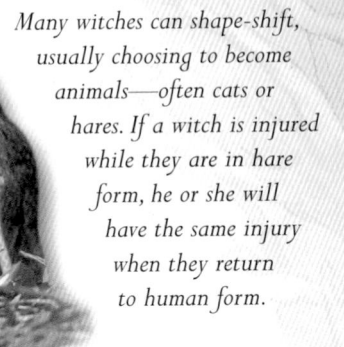

Many witches can shape-shift, usually choosing to become animals—often cats or hares. If a witch is injured while they are in hare form, he or she will have the same injury when they return to human form.

THE POWERS OF WITCHES

Witches are not usually born with magical powers. They must gain them by learning, by experimenting, or, it is said, by begging for them from the devil himself. However, they can be born with natural abilities, and the seventh son of a seventh son, or the seventh daughter of a seventh daughter, will have an instinctive talent for making spells.

The idea that most witches work for the devil is widespread, but some say that it is untrue—a misunderstanding made by the early Christian church, which was responsible for torturing and even burning alive those people suspected of witchcraft from the A.D. 300s to the 1700s.

The medieval ducking stool was one way of testing if someone was a witch. The suspect was strapped into the chair, which was then submerged in the water. A witch would survive—and then be killed. Anyone who drowned was declared innocent—and also dead.

WITCH MARKS

Witches who worked for the devil were said to carry marks on their bodies as a type of seal of their pact with him. A witch mark could be a mole, a freckle, a scar, or a birthmark—all common features that could be found on any person. If a woman—no matter how innocent—was accused of witchcraft, she was examined, and any mark on her body was declared to be a witch's mark—and a definite sign of her guilt.

Female witches are not always old and ugly, they can be young and beautiful—like this one seen dancing with demons.

Famous witches and enchantresses

Enchantresses have something in common with elves—they are always born with their powers already within them. Few are entirely human, and the enchantress-goddess Circe does not have any mortal blood in her at all. Witches are usually human, and their powers are the gifts of dark forces or the result of studying and experimentation. However, the most famous of the witches, Hecate, is purely a supernatural being.

CIRCE

Circe (left), the daughter of the Greek sun god Helios, lives on an island. When sailors are lured ashore by her singing—which is as beautiful as that of the Sirens—she uses her enchantment to turn them into animals. Long ago she transformed Odysseus' crew into pigs, but with the help of Hermes, Odysseus compelled her to return them to human form. Circe fell in love with him, persuaded him to stay for one year, and before he left, taught him how to save himself and his men from the songs of the Sirens and the dangers of Scylla and Charybdis (see pages 72–73).

*Baba Yaga with a mortar and pestle—
and a birch broom to sweep away her tracks.*

BABA YAGA

Baba Yaga is a horrifying Russian cannibal witch. Her favorite victims are children. She likes to cook and eat them and crunch on their bones. She lives deep within the Russian forest in a little hut that spins around on chickens' legs, surrounded by a fence made out of human skulls on spikes. She travels in a mortar—a type of bowl used for grinding up herbs—and paddles her way through the air with a pestle—which is the instrument used to grind the herbs. Wherever Baba Yaga flies, terrible storms and tempests follow.

MORGAN LE FAY

Stories of Morgan le Fay, or Morgana, are written in Celtic mythology and in the tales of King Arthur, the legendary King of Great Britain. She is sometimes described as the fairy queen of the magical land of Avalon, occasionally as a river goddess, often as King Arthur's sister, and sometimes as the Morrigan (see pages 124–125). She is a frightening and cruel figure who, according to some legends, tried to kill King Arthur and frighten his queen, Guinevere, to death.

HECATE

The queen of the witches, as well as a goddess of the underworld, Hecate is a figure of darkness who haunts graveyards and awakens phantoms to terrify the living. She is a triple goddess, and in pictures and statues she usually has three faces—and sometimes three joined bodies as well. The faces may be human, showing her as young, middle-aged, and very old. Sometimes though, one face is of a woman, one of a dog, and one of a horse.

This mask of Rangda, the evil witch goddess of Indonesian mythology, is carried in Balinese ceremonial dances.

FAMOUS WITCHES AND ENCHANTRESSES IN BOOKS

📖 *The Castle of Llyr*
Lloyd Alexander

📖 *The Dream Stealer*
Gregory Maguire

📖 *Winter of the Ice Wizard*
Mary Pope Osborne

📖 *Old Peter's Russian Tales*
Arthur Ransome

Spells, cauldrons, and familiars

Certain things have been associated with witches for hundreds of years—especially the witches of Europe and North America. They are the witches' equipment—used for flying, brewing potions, and working their spells. In addition to their knowledge of magic, witches share with wizards their understanding of spells. There are thousands of possible spells, varying greatly in strength and purpose—and, like any power, they can be used for good or evil.

BROOMSTICKS

The belief that witches can fly is ancient and widespread. The traditional witch's broom, or besom, was the standard household brush for hundreds of years, used by most people to sweep their floors. Witches fly, but they have no wings so they must have something to ride on to carry them through the sky. Almost all witches worked from their own homes, and as a broom was always handy, it became their chosen vehicle.

CAULDRONS

Originally cauldrons were nothing more sinister than large, rounded pots that stood or hung over a hearth fire to cook food. Just as a witch would use whatever was close at hand to ride on, the domestic cauldron was used to brew bewitching mixtures—among them love potions and brews designed to poison, heal, or make someone invisible.

Medieval pictures show witches on broomsticks, and even male witches riding pitchforks. Both brooms and pitchforks were common in countryside homes.

FAMILIARS

The witches of fantasy—whether good or evil—are often accompanied by animal familiars, usually cats. In medieval times it was believed that all witches worked for the devil, and it was he who provided the familiar—a demon in animal form—to carry messages between himself and the witch. This familiar might be an owl, a toad, or a goat, but most often it was a cat. So during the years when witches were hunted, innocent old women with pet cats were in serious danger.

WITCHES' HATS

Only witches in Europe and North America wear pointed hats; on other continents they have long, wild hair or head scarves. One possible explanation is that in England in the 1500s many countrywomen wore pointed hats, and the fashion may have lingered among the rural wonder-working women, who healed the ills of humans and animals.

Another theory is that the early Quakers wore similar hats, and in the late 1600s many were falsely accused of witchcraft. Finally it may be that the pointed hat was actually a cone of power (see page 96).

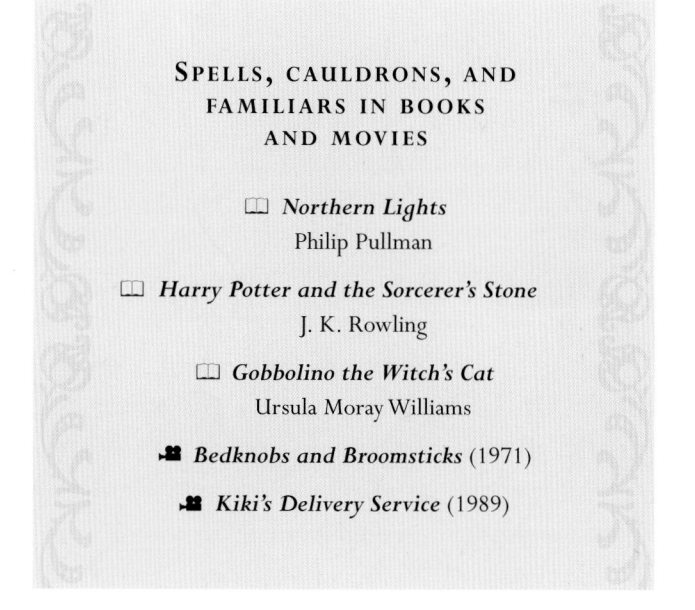

Even when most households had stoves and saucepans with handles, the witch of fantasy continued to use her traditional cauldron, or cooking pot, in which to create her various magical brews.

SPELLS, CAULDRONS, AND FAMILIARS IN BOOKS AND MOVIES

📖 *Northern Lights*
Philip Pullman

📖 *Harry Potter and the Sorcerer's Stone*
J. K. Rowling

📖 *Gobbolino the Witch's Cat*
Ursula Moray Williams

🎬 *Bedknobs and Broomsticks* (1971)

🎬 *Kiki's Delivery Service* (1989)

Wizards and magicians

Wizard means "wise"—a respecter and keeper
of knowledge. A wizard is usually kind and learned,
a worker of magic who may also be an alchemist,
astrologer, and creator of entertaining illusions and party magic.
The word magician is used in two very different ways—for
someone who practices dangerous magic, and for someone
who performs harmless magic tricks on a stage. Sometimes,
though, the two titles are used interchangeably.

*In ancient Rome the
Greek god Hermes was
called Mercury. The Mercury
caduceus, which symbolized
wisdom and healing, has
been used as a sign by
physicians and pharmacists
for hundreds of years.*

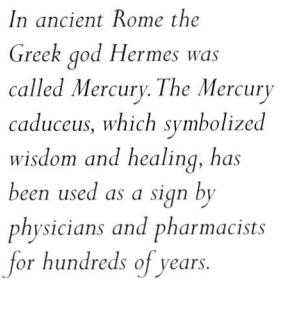

*Cones made out of beaten
gold and decorated with
crescent moons and sun
symbols have been discovered
by archaeologists in various
parts of Europe—this one
was found in Germany. The
cones were worn by Bronze
Age king-priests and are
the earliest known examples
of a wizard's pointed hat.*

WANDS AND STAFFS

Throughout history wands and staffs
have been used as symbols of power.
Kings and queens carry scepters, Christian
bishops have a ceremonial shepherd's crook,
and Hermes the Greek messenger-god and
magician carried a caduceus—a herald's wand
with two serpents entwining it. The wand of
a wizard or magician symbolizes power, but
if it is cut from the wood of a specially chosen
tree and prepared with the appropriate rituals,
it contains power within itself and is an
essential tool of the wizard's magical craft.

ALCHEMY AND ASTROLOGY

Most wizards are also alchemists and astrologers. Alchemists were the earliest chemists, best known for their attempts to create an elixir of life that would bestow immortality on anyone who drank it and for their efforts to produce a philosopher's stone to turn imperfect metals into perfect gold. However, they carried out many other experiments, and their main goal was to gain knowledge and wisdom with the hope of perfecting themselves.

Astrologers believe that the moon and the planets have a powerful effect on life on earth, and their positions at the exact moment of a person's birth reveal a lot about personality and destiny. Astronomer-wizards used the astronomical symbols on their hats and cloaks as charts that enabled them to predict the best times for sowing and reaping harvests.

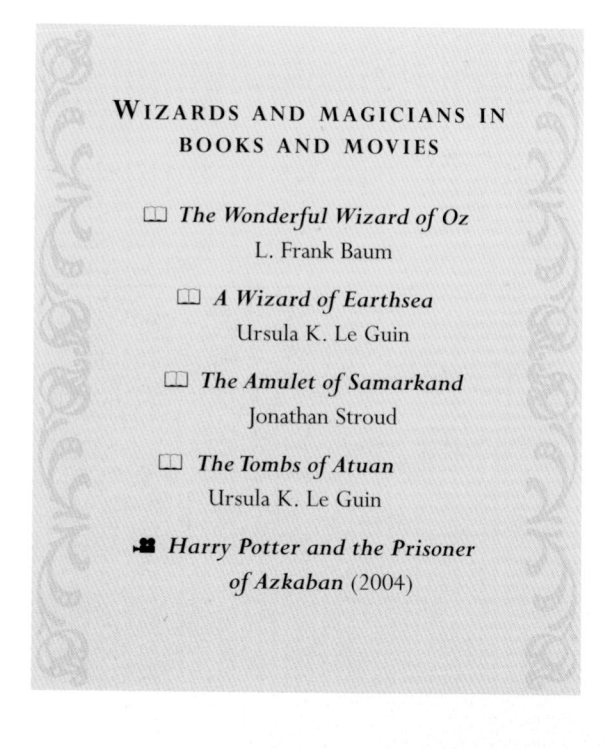

WIZARDS AND MAGICIANS IN BOOKS AND MOVIES

📖 *The Wonderful Wizard of Oz*
L. Frank Baum

📖 *A Wizard of Earthsea*
Ursula K. Le Guin

📖 *The Amulet of Samarkand*
Jonathan Stroud

📖 *The Tombs of Atuan*
Ursula K. Le Guin

🎥 *Harry Potter and the Prisoner of Azkaban* (2004)

The straight lines of runes make them suitable for carving into stone.

RUNES

In the world of fantasy rune means "magic sign," but runes were originally the letters of the earliest Germanic alphabet, used from the A.D. 200s by Anglo-Saxons and Scandinavians. Runic script, which is now only understood by a few, is one way of keeping the wizard's work secret so that it cannot be used by those who would not know how to handle it. Runes also add mystery to the magic of a spell or charm, just like riddles add mystery to the magic of the words of oracles and sphinxes (see pages 78–79).

Notable wizards

There are many famous wizard-magicians in fantasy, history, and myths and legends. Often the tales of their lives and their work have changed in the telling over hundreds of years, until it is no longer possible to know how and where they began. Some, such as John Dee, were human; others, such as Merlin, were only part-human; and Gwydion and Hermes Trismegistus may have been entirely supernatural beings.

JOHN DEE

An astrologer, mathematician, alchemist, and student of the occult, John Dee (1527–1608) was highly educated and so good at conjuring tricks that some thought that he was in league with the devil. At one time he was accused of witchcraft. However, he became an adviser and secret diplomatic agent to Queen Elizabeth I, and during her reign he was safe from persecution. Although he once claimed that he had succeeded in transforming common metal into gold, he died a poor man.

MERLIN

The stories that surround the great wizard Merlin (left) are as many and as complex as the spells that he wove. It is said that he had a human mother, but that his father was a demon from whom he inherited the gift of prophecy. His studies of magic were deep, and one of his great credits was causing some of the huge rocks from which Stonehenge was built to travel all the way from Wales. However, Merlin was baptized, and he never used sorcery or black magic. He is probably best known as the wise guide and teacher of King Arthur.

GWYDION

Gwydion was a wise, powerful, and knowledgeable Welsh wizard from Celtic mythology. His magical powers were strong, and he was a poet as well as a messenger to the gods, like the Greek Hermes and the Roman Mercury.

Stonehenge is a prehistoric monument on Salisbury Plain in Wiltshire, England. At dawn on Midsummer Day the sun strikes the altar stone—it is thought that the whole structure was used as a giant calendar to chart the sun's progress through the sky.

Hermes Trismegistus is said to have been the first alchemist, whose knowledge was greater than that of all the other alchemists combined.

NOTABLE WIZARDS IN BOOKS AND MOVIES

📖 ***The Seeing Stone***
Kevin Crossley-Holland

📖 ***Welsh Legends and Folk Tales***
Gwyn Jones

📖 ***The Once and Future King***
T. H. White

🎥 ***Merlin*** (1998)

🎥 ***The Sword in the Stone*** (1963)

HERMES TRISMEGISTUS

Hermes Trismegistus, whose name means "three times as great as Hermes," was a magician, a mystic, an alchemist, and an astrologer whose collected writings are known as the *Hermetica*. He is said to have had all the powers of Hermes—the Greek messenger to the gods and lord of magic—and also of Thoth—the Egyptian god of wisdom and magic. He may have been a mythical figure, or possibly there was a series of wizards and alchemists who used the name, and perhaps the writings of the *Hermetica* are the work of many people.

Sorcerers and necromancers

Sorcerers and necromancers are practitioners of the dark arts. Their magic is rarely benevolent and usually dangerous. It is risky to seek help from either one. Sorcerers do not worship the devil—or indeed anyone—because they want all the power for themselves. However, they may strike a deal with him. Necro is the Greek word for "corpse," and a necromancer is someone who raises the dead as assistants.

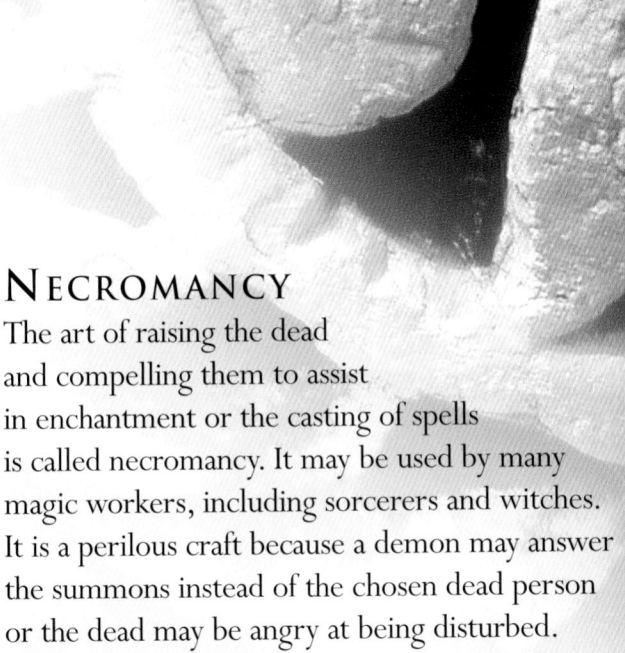

A grimoire is a sorcerer's handbook, containing recipes for potions, instructions for rituals, and designs for magical symbols and images. They are rare and ancient and often written in codes because at many times in many countries magic was illegal—and often punishable by death.

SORCERY

All workers of magic are seeking some type of power—the power to foretell the future, to heal, to harm, or to influence events. Many intend to use their power for good ends. But those who practice sorcery desire total and absolute power. Sorcery is not fundamentally about doing good or evil; it is about developing a power so mighty that it can even influence the stars in the sky. Sorcery is about attempting to rule the universe.

NECROMANCY

The art of raising the dead and compelling them to assist in enchantment or the casting of spells is called necromancy. It may be used by many magic workers, including sorcerers and witches. It is a perilous craft because a demon may answer the summons instead of the chosen dead person or the dead may be angry at being disturbed.

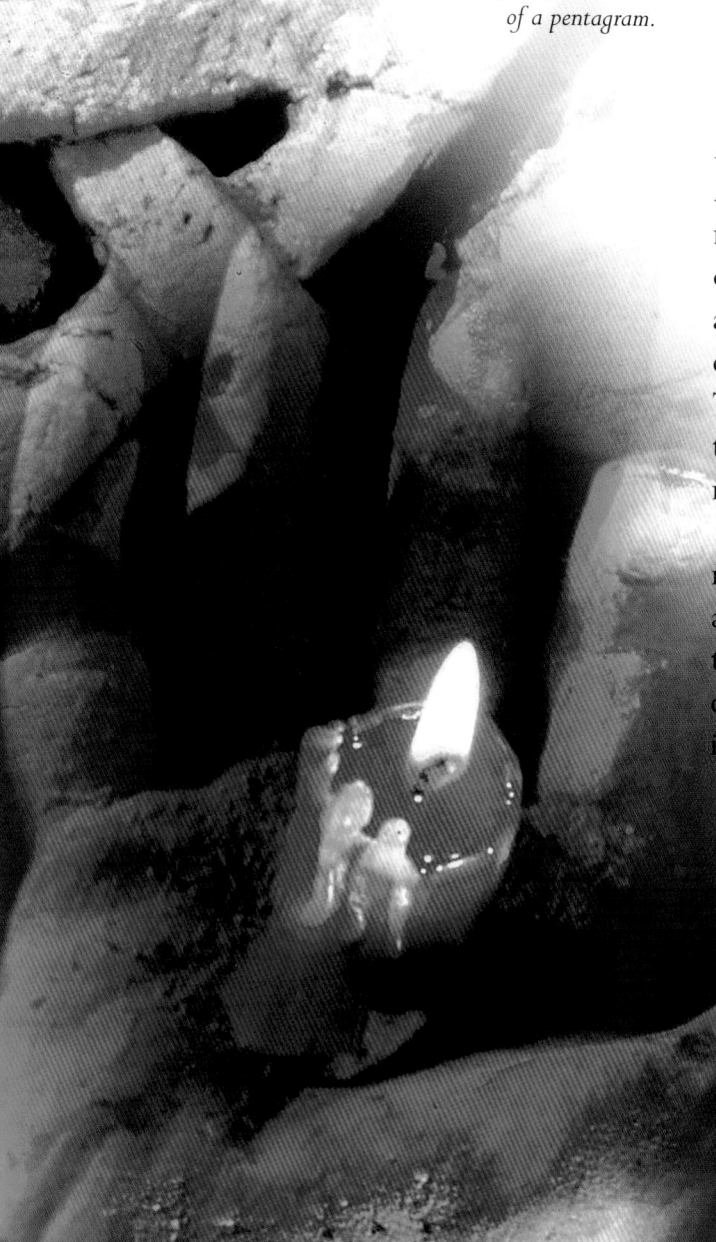

THE POWER OF NAMES

Sorcerers and witches are not the only ones who understand the importance of names— elves know it too. Possessing a person's true name is essential for gaining power over him or her. It is unwise to allow a worker of magic to know your true name—it should only be given to those who are trusted and trustworthy. This works both ways, and the Little People are usually careful to keep their real names secret from humans.

The five-pointed star of a pentagram.

SORCERERS AND NECROMANCERS IN BOOKS AND MOVIES

📖 ***The High King***
Lloyd Alexander

📖 ***The Farthest Shore***
Ursula K. Le Guin

📖 ***Sabriel***
Garth Nix

📖 ***Shadowmancer***
G. P. Taylor

🎥 ***The Black Cauldron*** (1985)

MAGIC CIRCLES AND SQUARES

A magic circle protects the sorcerer or magician who stands within it, because demons and spirits can only enter if they are invited. A magic square is a device for creating magic and for summoning spirits. The designs used are precise and elaborate, their positioning is crucial, and complex rituals accompany their construction.

The pentagram is one of the best-known magic symbols. *Penta* means "five," and a pentagram is a five-pointed star with the single point at the top. It is sometimes called a pentacle, but in fact a pentacle is any magic symbol or pattern.

The so-called Hand of Glory is a dried or mummified human hand that is used as a candleholder by sorcerers and necromancers. It is supposed to have the ability to paralyze all who see it so that they cannot move, speak, or run away.

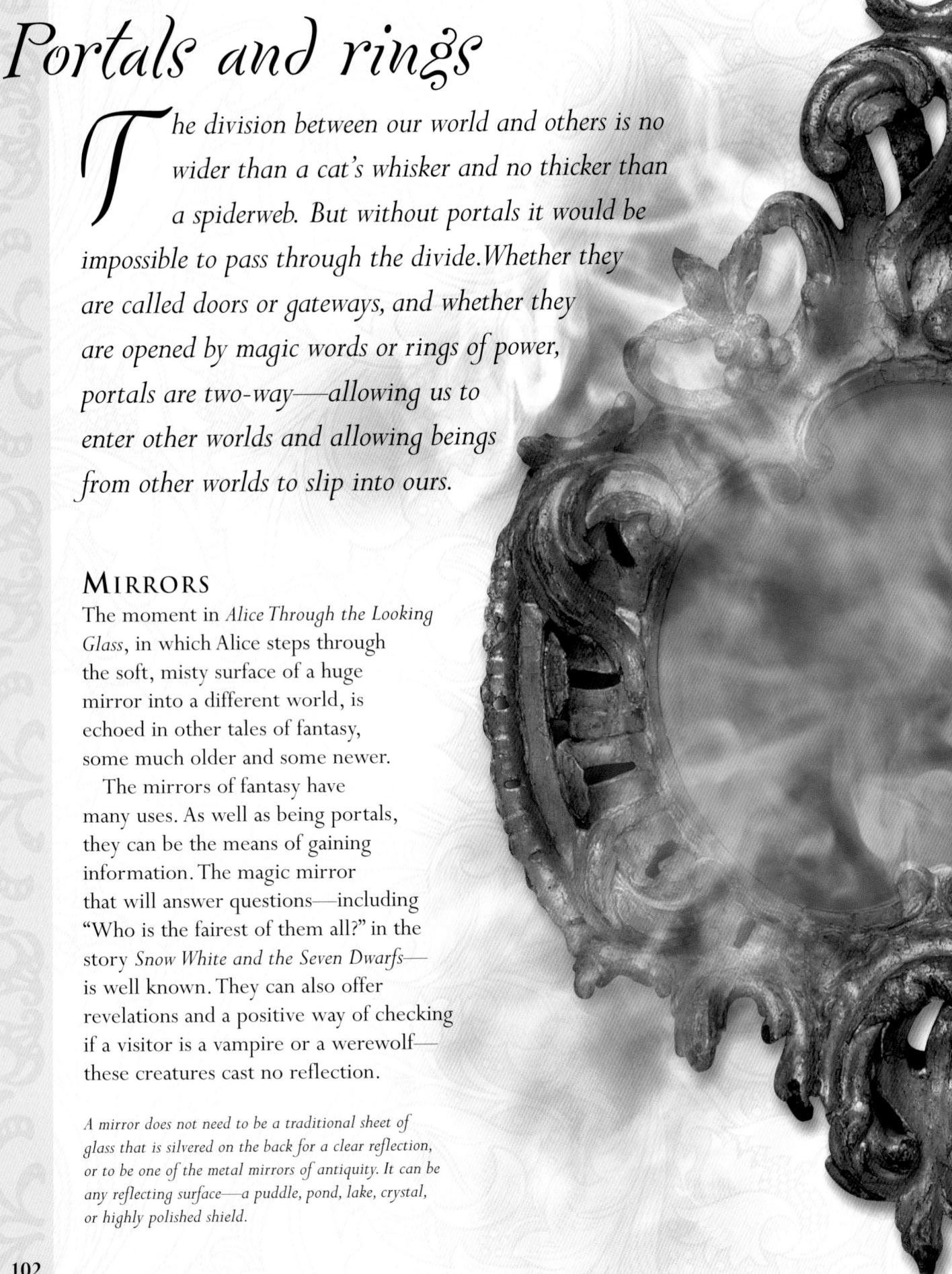

Portals and rings

The division between our world and others is no wider than a cat's whisker and no thicker than a spiderweb. But without portals it would be impossible to pass through the divide. Whether they are called doors or gateways, and whether they are opened by magic words or rings of power, portals are two-way—allowing us to enter other worlds and allowing beings from other worlds to slip into ours.

MIRRORS

The moment in *Alice Through the Looking Glass*, in which Alice steps through the soft, misty surface of a huge mirror into a different world, is echoed in other tales of fantasy, some much older and some newer.

The mirrors of fantasy have many uses. As well as being portals, they can be the means of gaining information. The magic mirror that will answer questions—including "Who is the fairest of them all?" in the story *Snow White and the Seven Dwarfs*—is well known. They can also offer revelations and a positive way of checking if a visitor is a vampire or a werewolf—these creatures cast no reflection.

A mirror does not need to be a traditional sheet of glass that is silvered on the back for a clear reflection, or to be one of the metal mirrors of antiquity. It can be any reflecting surface—a puddle, pond, lake, crystal, or highly polished shield.

OTHER DOORWAYS

Certain caves, ancient barrows, and other openings into hillsides are traditional entrances into the lands of the elves. Sometimes a portal is nothing more than a shadowy gap in the fabric of the universe—something sensed rather than seen. A few portals have fierce guardians. The three-headed dog, Cerberus (see pages 68–69), guards the opening to the underworld kingdom of Hades, and some believe that the purpose of lake monsters is to guard an entrance to another, secret universe.

PORTALS AND RINGS IN BOOKS AND MOVIES

- 📖 *Alice Through the Looking Glass*
  Lewis Carroll

- 📖 *The Lion, the Witch, and the Wardrobe*
  C. S. Lewis

- 📖 *The Lord of the Rings*
  J. R. R. Tolkien

- 🎥 *Harry Potter and the Sorcerer's Stone* (2001)

- 🎥 *Snow White and the Seven Dwarfs* (1937)

RINGS OF POWER

The earliest stories of rings of power, created by and usually owned by magicians, are incredibly ancient. Perhaps the most famous of these rings is the one that, according to legend, was owned by King Solomon. Belief in this ring may date back to the A.D. 300s, but possibly even earlier. Solomon was the great and wise king of Israel, described in the Old Testament, but the story of the magic ring does not come from the Bible but from elsewhere. Legend says that he used it when he was building the Temple of Jerusalem in order to gain power over the demons who tried to destroy it.

Since then there have been many tales of rings that contained the power to control demons, humans, and other beings— or to unlock the portals into other worlds.

Amulets, talismans, and charms

Traditionally an amulet is a magical object that already contains power within itself. A talisman is an object that has had its power put into it from an outside force. A charm is spoken or written, and if written, it may be in words or in symbols. As time has passed the meanings have become blurred and the words used interchangeably. But a magical object can be given extra power by the addition of a charm, and so it can be all three at once.

The Eye of Horus is a powerful amulet or charm against most types of evil, but especially the evil eye—a malevolent glance from a being with magical powers. Horus was the falcon-headed god of the ancient Egyptians.

SCARABS

The scarab is one of the most powerful of the ancient Egyptian amulets. The scarab is a beetle with beautiful, iridescent wing cases. It feeds on animal dung, which it first rolls into a ball. The female lays her egg within a buried dung ball. The egg hatches, and the grub grows and changes to emerge as an adult beetle, as if it were born from the earth. So the scarab is an emblem of resurrection (coming back to life). It is also a symbol of the sun because it is said to roll the ball from east to west, in imitation of the sun and the route of Ra, the Egyptian sun god.

Other cultures recognize power in different objects. Amulets are made from peach wood or peach stones in China. In Africa the wood of a sacred tree is used. People in many countries over hundreds of years credit crystals with healing properties. Even a stone, shaped and smoothed by water—especially if found in a sacred place—can be judged to be magical.

In New Zealand the Maori carve tikis out of jade to represent protective spirits, which are also called tikis.

LODESTONES

A lodestone is a naturally magnetic piece of rock containing iron ore, also known as magnetite. It attracts iron, and if suspended or balanced so that it can move, it will point to the magnetic poles of the earth. Its name comes from the Old English word *lod*, meaning "way"—so it is a way stone, an early form of compass. It is said to bestow strength and determination and to protect from all harm. Alexander the Great had lodestone amulets issued to each one of his soldiers.

AMULETS, TALISMANS, AND CHARMS IN BOOKS AND MOVIES

📖 *The Story of the Amulet*
E. Nesbit

📖 *The Amulet of Samarkand*
Jonathan Stroud

🎥 *Dungeons & Dragons* (2000)

🎥 *The Golden Voyage of Sinbad* (1974)

A dried scarab beetle, or a man-made likeness (opposite page, top left), is believed to bring fortune and health to the living, and when it is placed in a tomb, to bring eternal life to the dead. The scarab's likeness is made out of many materials, including gold and precious stones. Often a prayer or a charm is scratched on the underside.

*Two wizards locked in
battle may shape-shift many
times, each one trying to turn into
a stronger or more cunning species.*

CHAPTER SEVEN

Shape-shifters

Shape-shifting—or metamorphosis—is a magical transformation. Shape-shifters can change into different creatures or change size, becoming enormous or tiny at will. Those with this power include witches, wizards, shamans, demons, elves, and fairies. Some change themselves; some change others—perhaps to escape dange or perhaps to inflict terrible punishment.

Werewolves

The werewolf is possibly the most dramatic, terrifying, and famous of all shape-shifters. He is known throughout northern Europe, North America, and Canada. In fact, he is known wherever wolf packs have lived in the past or live now. Even in countries where the wolf has become extinct, the werewolf still raises his muzzle to the moon and howls. Other countries and other cultures have other "were-creatures"—South America has the werejaguar, China the weresnake, Africa and Australia have the werecrocodile, and India has the weretiger.

THE POWER OF WOLVES

Wolves are brave and loyal to their pack. They are good mothers, and not only to their own kind. There have been several cases of female wolves suckling and taking care of abandoned human infants. In spite of this, wolves are fierce, especially when they are hungry, and will easily make a meal of a child or a lone adult. In the past when most houses had flimsy wooden walls, a pack could easily break its way in. If the occupants had no guns, they had no way of protecting themselves. In such times the wolf seemed supernaturally powerful. Stories of shape-shifters were widespread, and it was a small step to the horrifying belief that a man—with his knowledge of people's homes, lives, and weaknesses—could become an even more deadly form of wolf.

In 1858 the Baroness Dudevant (better known as the French novelist George Sand) told her son about her sighting of a group of werewolves. Maurice, who also used the surname Sand, drew this picture based on her description.

SILVER BULLETS

In the time of the pagan wolf cults the wolf-man was often gentle and wise. The werewolf of fantasy, though, is always a ravenous beast, who will rip its victims' throats out with its strong jaws. The change from human to wolf takes place during a full moon—traditionally a time of magic and madness.

A man (and they usually are men) may become a werewolf because one has bitten him. It could be because he has used a magic ointment or has put on a wolf's pelt in order to change himself. Or it may be because he has been bewitched. If bewitched, he will return to his human form after nine years, provided he has not eaten human flesh during that time. When faced with a werewolf, the most effective weapons are iron or silver—the most convenient is a silver-tipped arrow or a silver bullet. The creature will always revert to its human shape as it dies.

WEREWOLVES IN BOOKS AND MOVIES

📖 *The Wereling*
Stephen Cole

📖 *The Wolving Time*
Patrick Jennings

📖 *The Golem's Eye*
Jonathan Stroud

🎥 *The 10th Kingdom* (2000)

🎥 *Harry Potter and the Prisoner of Azkaban* (2004)

Wer is Old English for "man," so werewolf (sometimes spelled werwolf) is a man-wolf. For a man to become a wolf, almost every part of his body must change. His hair and claws grow, and his teeth become larger and stronger. His head changes shape and develops a muzzle. His back becomes longer, shoulders flatten, and legs and arms reshape their bones.

Occasionally in the past people were
accidentally buried alive (something
that could not happen today with modern
medical techniques). If an opened grave
revealed a corpse whose struggles to
escape had left blood on their mouth
and fingernails, it was declared a vampire.

CHAPTER EIGHT

The undead

The undead are those individuals whose bodies and minds
are dead, but somehow—by magical and mysterious
means—they continue to function—and always with
evil intent. They include vampires, walking skeletons,
and zombies. Belief in these grisly and terrifying creatures
grew out of a fear that the dead might be jealous of
the living, and so they might choose to prey on them.

Vampires

Vampires are as old as recorded history. They are creatures of the night—blood-sucking shape-shifters who can change into smoke, mist, bats, wolves, dogs, or cats. In Japan it is the vampire cat of Nabeshima who is the most feared. Female vampires in India linger at crossroads to suck the blood of elephants. Vampire legends come from China, Egypt, Greece, Malaysia, Africa, the Americas, Arabia, and—perhaps especially—eastern Europe.

Vampire bats live in Central and South America and the West Indies. They make tiny incisions in the skin of their victims with their sharp teeth and then lap, rather than suck, the blood. Their animal or human victims never turn into bats or vampires.

As dawn breaks vampires must climb back into the safety of their coffins. During the daylight hours vampires are vulnerable to attacks from those who wish to destroy them.

EASTERN EUROPEAN VAMPIRES

Vampir is a Magyar, or Hungarian, word for "undead," and similar words are used in many eastern European languages. Another title is *Nosferatu*, which means "living corpse." Vampires cast no shadow and have no reflection. Folklore describes them as red-faced and unshaven, with loud voices, ever-open mouths, and pronounced canine teeth, or fangs. It also says that they leap on their victims and crush and smother them while sucking their blood. The pale, elegant, clean-shaven vampire—such as Count Dracula, who leaves two neat holes in a victim's neck—did not appear until the A.D. 1800s.

The common way to become a vampire is to be bitten by one, just as the most common way to become a werewolf is from a bite. In fact vampires are closely related to werewolves, and they often have wolves and bats in their power.

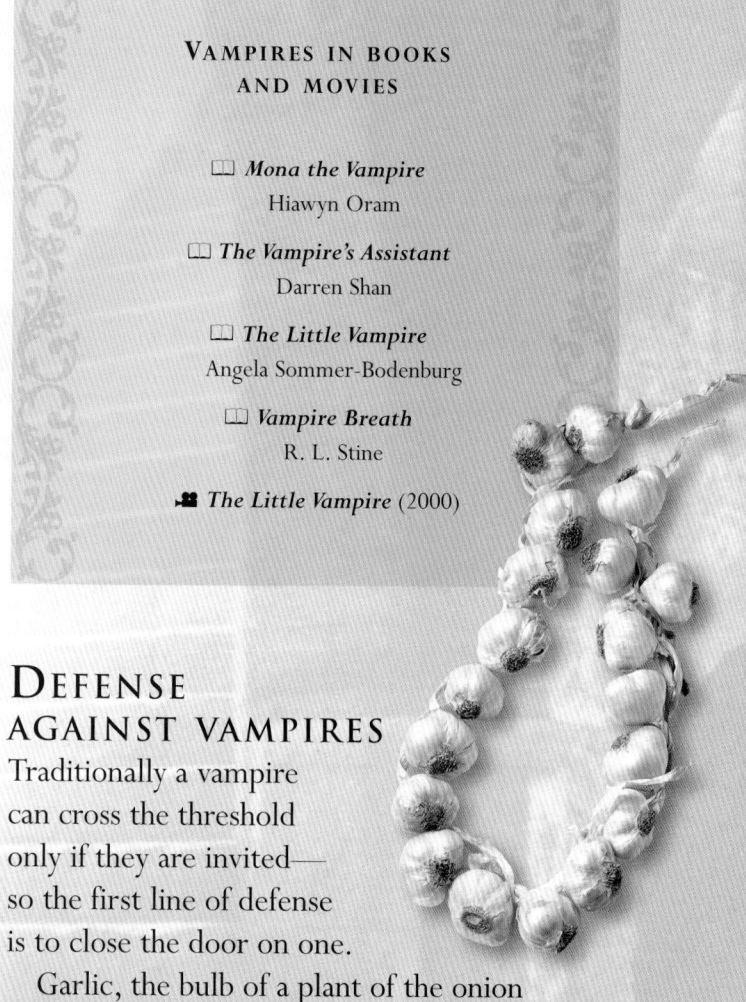

The two-tailed vampire cat of Nabeshima, Japan, kills by strangling, not biting. Her story tells that she murdered a princess, shape-shifted to look like her, and then preyed on the prince. Eventually she was caught and killed.

VAMPIRES IN BOOKS AND MOVIES

☐ *Mona the Vampire*
Hiawyn Oram

☐ *The Vampire's Assistant*
Darren Shan

☐ *The Little Vampire*
Angela Sommer-Bodenburg

☐ *Vampire Breath*
R. L. Stine

🎥 *The Little Vampire* (2000)

DEFENSE AGAINST VAMPIRES

Traditionally a vampire can cross the threshold only if they are invited—so the first line of defense is to close the door on one.

Garlic, the bulb of a plant of the onion family, which is often used in cooking, has been relied upon for centuries to ward off evil of all types—especially vampires. Medically, eating garlic can help prevent the blood from clotting, and you might think that vampires would find this appealing in a victim, but they do not. Iron and, to a lesser extent, silver are also deterrents. Vampires are active only between sunset and sunrise, so the daylight hours are safe. During those daylight hours they have to return to their coffins to rest. Finding the coffin and destroying both it and the vampire inside will bring the reign of terror to an end, but it is a messy task. Recommended methods are to drive a stake through the vampire's heart, or to behead it, or to burn the body. Some say that all three methods are necessary, but others say that any one of them will do the trick.

Count Dracula

In A.D. 1897 a book was published that changed people's ideas about vampires forever. *Dracula*, by the Irish author Bram (Abraham) Stoker, is not the earliest vampire story, but it is by far the most famous and the most influential. Other 19th-century authors wrote about pale and aristocratic vampires, but Bram Stoker's elegantly dressed count fixed this image in the collective imagination. It also confirmed the belief that the human vampire is able to shape-shift at will into a bat.

Most of Count Dracula's victims were young and beautiful women who, once they were bitten, were doomed to become vampires themselves.

DRACULA

In Bram Stoker's Gothic horror story
Count Dracula buys an ancient estate in
Great Britain. A young lawyer named Jonathan
Harker, whose diaries tell the story, travels to
the count's castle in Transylvania to arrange
matters. Among other dreadful experiences,
he discovers the count resting during the day in
his coffin in a ruined chapel. The count sails for
Whitby in Yorkshire, England, to his new estate,
taking his coffin and boxes of dirt from the
Dracula family graveyard with him. None
of the crew survives the voyage. In England
Harker and Professor van Helsing, an authority
on vampires who recognizes the true nature
of Dracula, struggle—with partial success—
to save Harker's fiancée and
her best friend from the
count's vampirish ways.
Eventually they pursue
him back to Transylvania
where they at last succeed
in beheading him and
stabbing him through
the heart—at which
point he turns into dust.

*This portrait of Vlad Dracula was painted by a German
artist in the A.D. 1500s. Vlad ruled Wallachia from
1456–1462, during which he earned his legendary
name, Vlad the Impaler, through a reign of terror.*

VLAD THE IMPALER

Dracula once existed, although he was not a
vampire. He was born in A.D. 1430, the son
of Prince Vlad of Wallachia. Wallachia is in
the southern part of Romania, not all that far
from Transylvania. Vlad was a member of the
distinguished Hungarian Order of the Dragon
and became known as Vlad Dracul, or Vlad the
Dragon. In Wallachian the words for dragon
and devil are the same, and as Vlad was a cruel
ruler the name was appropriate. The name
"Dracula" means young, or junior, Dracul,
so Vlad's son became Vlad Dracula. Even
worse than his father, he was also called Vlad
the Impaler because, it is said, he caused
more than 100,000 people to be impaled
on sharpened stakes as a form of execution.

The true story is the source of many
elements of the novel—the name, the
country, the cruelty, and the sharpened
stakes—although in the story the sharpened
stakes are used against the "devil," not by him.

COUNT DRACULA IN BOOKS

- *Vlad the Drac*
  Ann Jungman

- *Dracula's Tomb*
  Colin McNaughton

- *Dracula's Revenge*
  Gary Morecambe

- *Dracula*
  Mike Stocks

Skeletons and symbolic heads

Reverence for the head, detached from its body, goes back to the earliest civilizations. Real heads have been trophies of war, sources of wisdom, and protectors of realms. Heads carved out of wood or stone are found in almost every country. Skeletons, however, are symbols of death. To cultures that dread death, skeletons and skulls are always frightening. Skulls are especially eerie—and they have even been used as macabre drinking cups.

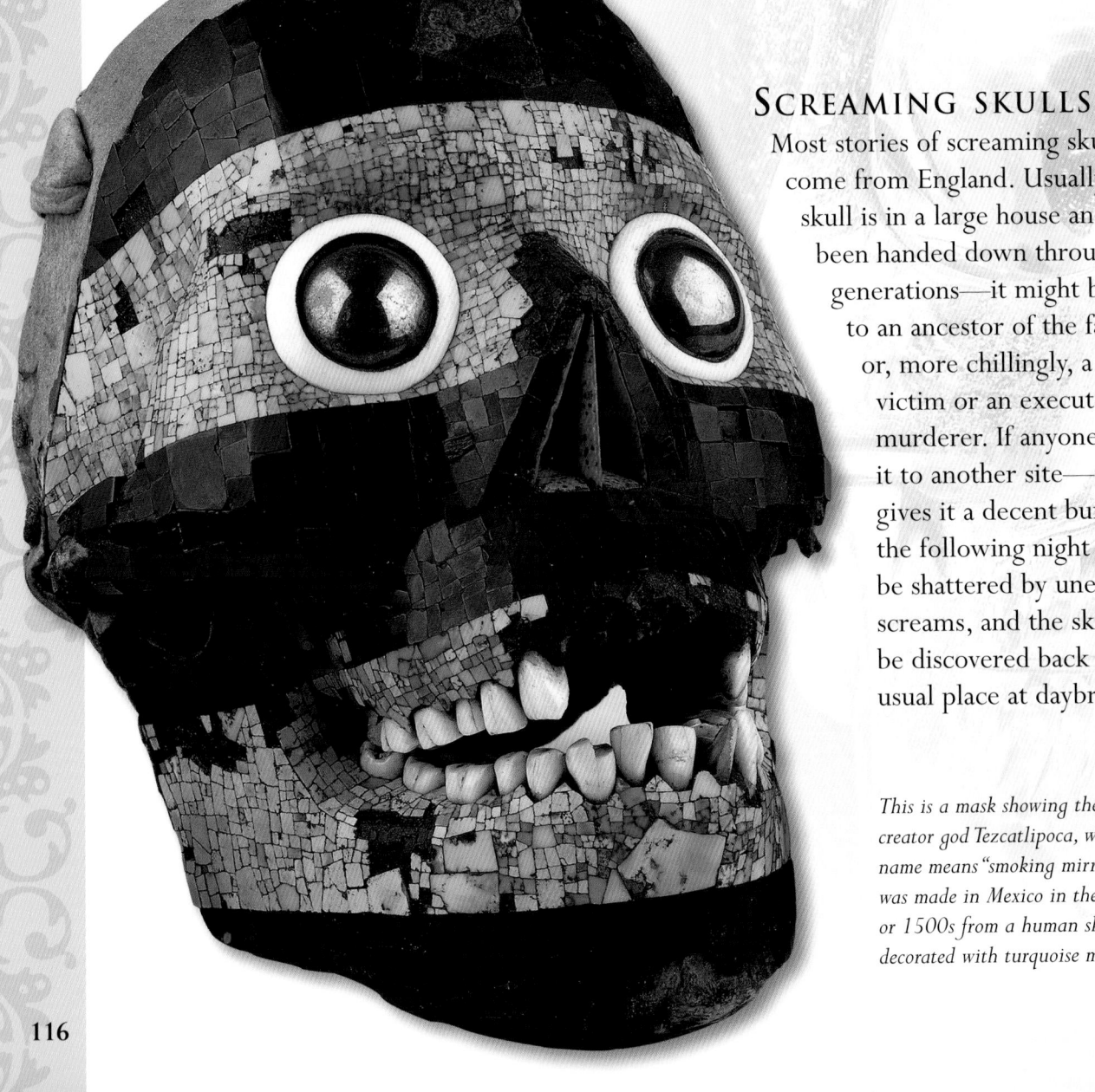

SCREAMING SKULLS

Most stories of screaming skulls come from England. Usually the skull is in a large house and has been handed down through generations—it might belong to an ancestor of the family or, more chillingly, a murder victim or an executed murderer. If anyone moves it to another site—or even gives it a decent burial— the following night will be shattered by unearthly screams, and the skull will be discovered back in its usual place at daybreak.

This is a mask showing the Aztec creator god Tezcatlipoca, whose name means "smoking mirror." It was made in Mexico in the 1400s or 1500s from a human skull decorated with turquoise mosaic.

116

SYMBOLIC HEADS

To those who believed that the head contained the spirit, even after death, the taking of a head was a way of claiming some of the energy and power of the owner. Generations ago head-hunting was a common practice in Amazonia, New Guinea, India, the Philippines, and the Solomon Islands. The Jivaro, a fierce people of Ecuador, shrunk the severed heads of their opponents to trap their souls and prevent them from taking revenge.

Bran the Blessed, a great mythic king of Great Britain, ordered that his head be buried in the White Hill in London—where the Tower of London now stands—to protect against invaders. It is rumored to have been removed to a safer, secret place by King Arthur, but Bran's sacred birds, the ravens, still live at the Tower and protect the country.

THE DAY OF THE DEAD

Skeletons are not always frightening or sinister. On the Mexican Day of the Dead—*Dia de los Muertos*—there are fantasy images of death and skeletons everywhere, but it is a happy occasion. It is a massive family reunion to honor the benevolent dead, ancestors, and friends who are gone but not forgotten. Personal altars hold their images, surrounded by the things that they loved when they were alive. There are candles everywhere, as well as marigolds—the flowers of the dead. The festival goes back to 3,500 B.C., although its ancient traditions blended with Christianity when the Spanish conquistadores arrived in the A.D. 1500s. Although it begins on October 31, it is much older than Halloween and separate from it.

Skulls, such as this one, are made out of sugar for children to eat during the Mexican Day of the Dead.

SKELETONS AND SYMBOLIC HEADS IN BOOKS AND MOVIES

- *Charlie Eggleston's Talking Skull* Bruce Coville
- *How I Got My Shrunken Head* R. L. Stine
- *The Crystal Skulls* Jan Visser
- *Jason and the Argonauts* (1963)
- *Vice Versa* (1988)

117

Mummies, zombies, and golems

In fantasy zombies and golems are powered by a magician who controls them from a distance—often with evil intentions. Mummies are powered by their own anger toward those who have disturbed their tombs. All of them are strong and terrifying. It is hopeless to reason with them and impossible to kill them— mummies and zombies because they are already dead, and golems because they were never truly alive.

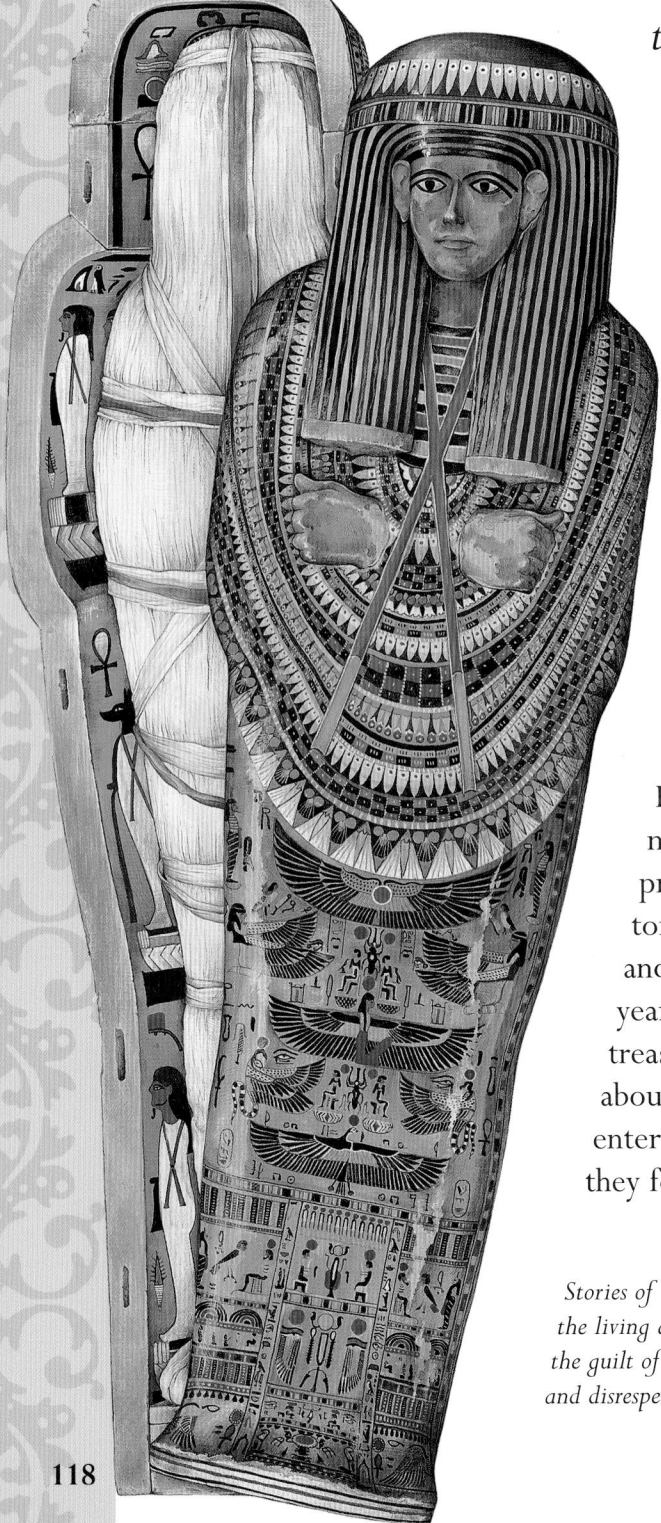

MUMMIES

The preserved body of a human or an animal is called a mummy. Bodies can be naturally preserved in ice or in desert sand, but several early civilizations deliberately preserved their dead. They removed the internal organs, protected the skin with oils, and bound the body in cloth. The most famous were the ancient Egyptians. Their royal families and priests were mummified, placed in beautiful coffins with protective amulets, and then buried in elaborate tombs or pyramids—with supplies of food, drinks, and valuables for the afterlife. For hundreds of years, despite stories of ancient curses, the buried treasures attracted thieves. In addition, curiosity about ancient Egypt tempted archaeologists to enter pyramids, remove and examine whatever they found, and, usually, place it in museums.

Stories of vengeful mummies attacking the living almost certainly come from the guilt of those who have robbed and disrespected them.

118

ZOMBIES

A sorcerer creates a zombie by reanimating a corpse, which is then used to threaten or attack his or her victims. The first zombies were in Haiti, as part of the Haitian voodoo cult. Later zombies loomed out of misty, imaginary lands. None of them has any will of their own. Supposedly if they eat salty food or look at the sea, they will return to their graves.

GOLEMS

A golem (below) is a manlike figure made of mud or clay and activated by spells and by a special word written either on its forehead or on a parchment that is placed inside of its mouth. One of the words used is *emeth*, meaning "life." When the word is removed, the golem collapses—on at least one occasion crushing its master. The most famous golem maker, according to legend, was the Rabbi of Prague, Judah Loew ben Bezaleel (1525–1609). He used a golem as a servant but always carefully rested it on a Friday so that it would be still during the Sabbath (Saturday). One day he forgot and only just had time to stop it by removing the parchment from the golem's mouth as it made its way toward the synagogue. The figure turned to dust, and its remains are said to lie in the synagogue's attic.

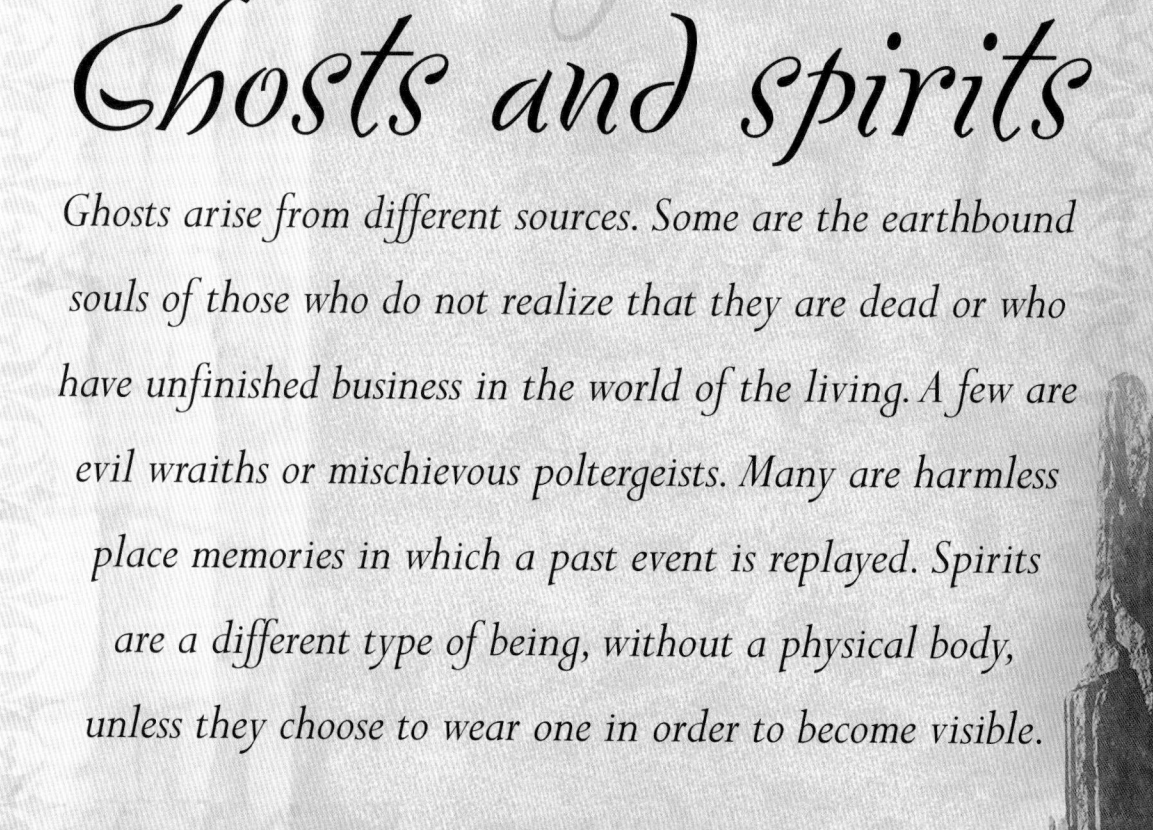

CHAPTER NINE

Ghosts and spirits

Ghosts arise from different sources. Some are the earthbound souls of those who do not realize that they are dead or who have unfinished business in the world of the living. A few are evil wraiths or mischievous poltergeists. Many are harmless place memories in which a past event is replayed. Spirits are a different type of being, without a physical body, unless they choose to wear one in order to become visible.

Djinn or genies

The djinn who drifted into the world of fantasy through **The Thousand And One Nights,** *often known as* **The Arabian Nights,** *are very different from the djinn of Islam. These tales were told by Indian, Persian, and Arabian storytellers for several hundred years. They were first written down around* A.D. *850 in Arabic, reaching Europe in French translation in the early 1700s. Since then they have appeared in many languages.*

This painting shows Sinbad the sailor overwhelmed by the enormous genie he has released from its imprisoning jar.

THE NAMES OF THE DJINN

In Arabic they are djinn or jinn in the plural and djinni or jinni in the singular. In French and English they are usually genies in the plural and genie in the singular. These are all names for the same creatures, which are created from fire and can take any shape they choose—animal or human—and can be of any size, including gigantic and awe-inspiring. It is said that most are hostile, although some can be friendly. It is possible for magicians or wise men and women to gain power over djinn and to use them to perform amazing and magical tasks. Like the Little People, even friendly djinn can be unpredictable, and certainly anyone who breaks an agreement with djinn will strongly regret it.

In all there are five different types. The least powerful is the jann, next come the djinn (which is also the overall name for all five), and then the sheytans, or devils. The afrits, sometimes called efreets, are very powerful, but the marids are the most powerful and dangerous of all.

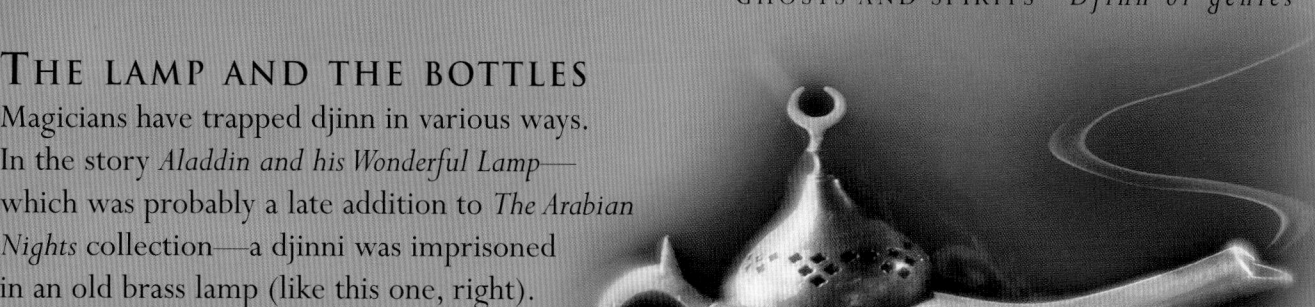

THE LAMP AND THE BOTTLES

Magicians have trapped djinn in various ways. In the story *Aladdin and his Wonderful Lamp*—which was probably a late addition to *The Arabian Nights* collection—a djinni was imprisoned in an old brass lamp (like this one, right). Rubbing the lamp released the djinni, and it would obey whoever set it free.

Traditionally it is said that the great and wise King Solomon shut misbehaving djinn in lead-stoppered bottles and threw them into the sea. Sometimes these were caught in fishnets. Any person who opened a bottle might be granted three wishes or, more likely, would find the freed spirit so dangerous that it was wiser to trick it into reentering the bottle, which could be closed securely and thrown back.

Traditionally King Solomon's flying carpet could carry his entire court, but most flying carpets were just like any beautiful handwoven rugs until they were powered into flight by magic.

DJINN OR GENIES IN BOOKS AND MOVIES

📖 *The Twelve and the Genii*
Pauline Clarke

📖 *The Akhenaten Adventure*
P. B. Kerr

📖 *The Amulet of Samarkand*
Jonathan Stroud

🎥 *Aladdin* (1992)

🎥 *Arabian Nights* (2000)

Messengers of death

Death is a mystery that has been solved in different ways by the religions, mythologies, and fantasies of every civilization. One of the ideas found in the most ancient stories—and still believed by many today—is that the moment when the Fates cut the thread of a life can be foreseen. If the time of death can be known, then it follows that a death messenger may bring a warning.

The washerwoman at the ford is called the Bean Nighe in Gaelic. She is found in the lands of the Celts crouching by a ford or pool, washing the clothes of those whose death is close. If a passing mortal asks politely, she will tell the names of the chosen.

THE FETCH

The fetch is a living ghost, the wraithlike image of a person who will die soon. It may be seen by relations or close friends—or by the person themselves. In the dark of night it appears only as a small flame—known as a fetch light—and may be confused with other phantom lights.

In Irish tradition the fetch only foretells death if it appears at night. If a fetch is seen in the morning, it predicts a long life.

MESSENGERS OF DEATH IN BOOKS

📖 *The Weirdstone of Brisingamen*
Alan Garner

📖 *The Hounds of the Morrigan*
Pat O'Shea

📖 *Halloween Pie*
Michael O. Tunnell

📖 *Harry Potter and the Prisoner of Azkaban*
J. K. Rowling

THE BANSHEE

Her name comes from the Gaelic
Bean Sidhe, meaning "a woman of the
fairies" or "a female spirit." Her wailing
voice is heard when death is close. Each
banshee is attached to an Irish family
or clan, and she only cries for one of her
own. Traditionally her keening is heard
around the ancestral home—even if the
one who is dying is far away—and the
sound indicates the type of death—low
and soft for peaceful passing, and harsh
and high for a violent end. It is also said
that only aristocratic families have banshees
and that a person of lowly birth who hears
a banshee's lament has nothing to fear.

DOPPELGÄNGERS

The name doppelgänger means "double-goer"
in German and is more often translated as
double-walker or cowalker. Like the fetch,
it is an exact replica of a specific human
being, and it is usually believed that
to see one's own doppelgänger
is to receive warning that
death is close. Certainly
the French writer Guy de
Maupassant (1850–1893)
said that he saw his
doppelgänger toward
the end of his life, and it is
said that both Queen Elizabeth I
(1533–1603) and the English poet
Percy Bysshe Shelley (1792–1822) saw
theirs shortly before their deaths. However,
there are cases where—either because of
a wrinkle in time or because some people
are able to project images of themselves—
a doppelgänger has been seen by several
people, but the person it represents has
continued to live for many years.

*The Morrigan is the great queen of the Tuatha
Dé Danaan, the ancient Irish gods whose descendants
are the Little People. She is a shape-shifter—sometimes
she is a beautiful warrior goddess and sometimes a wolf or a
crow. On a battlefield she is a shrieking, ancient hag, leaping
around the killing fields, choosing which soldiers will die.*

Ghouls and evil spirits

Ghouls are ancient creatures of horror and fantasy. They share with other evil spirits—including boggarts, goblins, imps, wights, and the mara—a desire to bring terror and danger to human beings. Traditionally they can be kept at bay by silver, by the sound of bells, and by a refusal to allow the mind to be ruled by fear.

Traditionally the ringing of church bells will drive away storms, plagues, demons, ghouls, and all other foul winds and dangerous creatures.

GHÛLS AND GHOULS

In Arabic folklore a ghûl is a monstrous, shape-shifting demon. It may take the form of a dog or a hyena (below) to open graves and feast on the bodies within. It also feeds on lost, lone travelers. In European fantasy ghouls are among the undead, one-time humans who have become ghouls by eating human flesh. They are hideous and give off a stench of rotting carrion. Although very strong, they are not intelligent, and it is easier for a human being to outwit them than to fight them.

Nightmares can be caused by guilt. Here, Ivan IV, who was crowned Czar (Emperor) of Russia in 1547, is visited by the angry ghosts of the men, women, and children that he murdered. He was a fierce ruler—often so cruel to his subjects that he became known as Ivan the Terrible.

NIGHTMARES

The mares of the night are not female horses, but demons known in Norse and Old English as mara or mera. They crouch on a sleeper's chest and bring bad dreams, originally called nightmaras or, in German, *alpdrücken*. At first the word only described dreams about crushing or suffocation, but since the early 1800s it has been used for any bad or frightening dream.

An evil imp is in the service of the devil. His greatest skill is spreading lies to create anxiety and confusion. His most powerful weapon is fear itself.

GOBLINS, BOGGARTS, AND IMPS

Boggarts and goblins are evil creatures that fall within the wide and varied group of elvish beings called the Little People. Imps are somewhat different. Their name comes from an Old English word meaning "young shoot," especially one that can be cut and used to grow a new plant. It can be used affectionately for a mischievous child, but in fantasy it usually means an offshoot of the devil himself.

WIGHTS

Wight comes from an Anglo-Saxon word *wiht*, which had several meanings, including "person" and "thing." It was sometimes used to refer to the spirit guardians of sacred places, who were called landvættir, or land wights, in Norse mythology. Originally they commanded respect rather than fear, but in more recent times they have been regarded as evil—especially since J. R. R. Tolkien wrote about the terrible barrow wights in *The Lord of the Rings*.

GHOULS AND EVIL SPIRITS IN BOOKS AND MOVIES

📖 ***One Thousand and One Nights***
Geraldine McCaughrean

📖 ***The Book of Nightmares***
John Peel

📖 ***The Lord of the Rings***
J. R. R. Tolkien

🎥 ***Harry Potter and the Prisoner of Azkaban*** (2004)

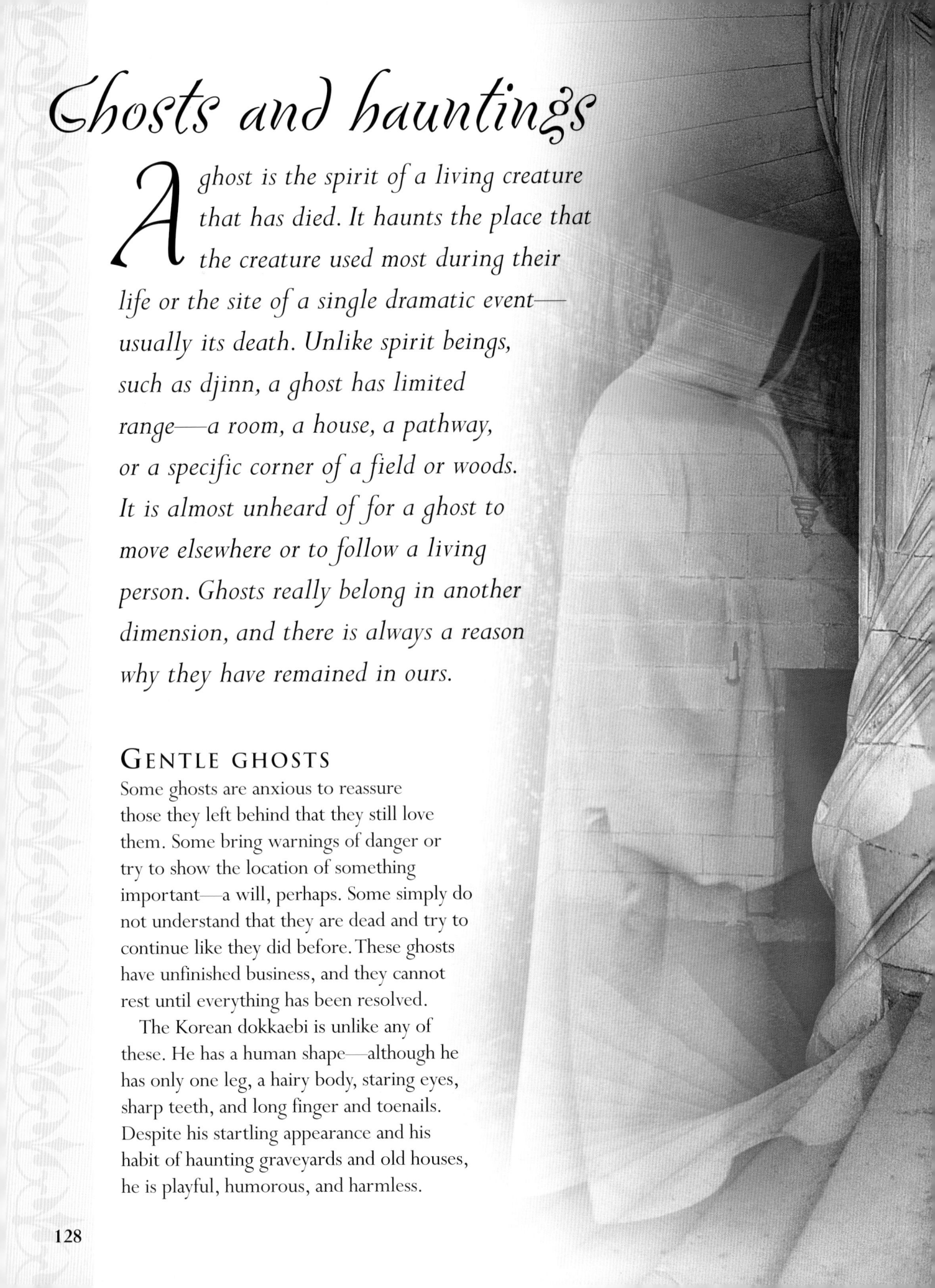

Ghosts and hauntings

A ghost is the spirit of a living creature that has died. It haunts the place that the creature used most during their life or the site of a single dramatic event—usually its death. Unlike spirit beings, such as djinn, a ghost has limited range—a room, a house, a pathway, or a specific corner of a field or woods. It is almost unheard of for a ghost to move elsewhere or to follow a living person. Ghosts really belong in another dimension, and there is always a reason why they have remained in ours.

GENTLE GHOSTS

Some ghosts are anxious to reassure those they left behind that they still love them. Some bring warnings of danger or try to show the location of something important—a will, perhaps. Some simply do not understand that they are dead and try to continue like they did before. These ghosts have unfinished business, and they cannot rest until everything has been resolved.

The Korean dokkaebi is unlike any of these. He has a human shape—although he has only one leg, a hairy body, staring eyes, sharp teeth, and long finger and toenails. Despite his startling appearance and his habit of haunting graveyards and old houses, he is playful, humorous, and harmless.

DRAMATIC HAUNTINGS

Many of the most frightening hauntings are by those who have been hanged, murdered, tortured, or walled up alive for their beliefs. Some may be place memories, but some are ghosts that are trapped at the site of their deaths by their own rage against the living who caused their suffering. These also have unfinished business, and they may be laid to rest if their bones are found and buried decently and their stories told.

PLACE MEMORY AND TIME SLIP

Certain places can "remember" or record events that have been repeated often. No one knows how or where the sights, and sometimes sounds, are recorded—in the fabric of buildings or in the rocks below the earth's surface—nor is it known what causes them to replay.

Time slip is when either the human witness slips back into the past or else a moment from the past slips into the present. A brief vision of an ancient army marching in the present-day world could be place memory. If, however, the visible world around the ancient army changes so that it also belongs in the distant past, the likely explanation is time slip.

Time slip is rare, and the human observer is warned not to try to change the past. Place memory is not uncommon, and the observer has no more power to change or affect anything than he or she could have on a movie.

GHOSTS IN BOOKS AND MOVIES

📖 *A Christmas Carol*
Charles Dickens

📖 *The Woman in Black*
Susan Hill

📖 *Macbeth*
William Shakespeare, Andrew Matthews

📖 *The Canterville Ghost*
Oscar Wilde

🎥 *Casper* (1995)

🎥 *Ghostbusters* (1984)

Poltergeists

A poltergeist is not an ordinary ghost, it's a form of energy—sometimes very violent energy. It seems likely that there is more than one type of poltergeist—and more than one cause. Poltergeist activity has been recorded all over the world for at least 2,000 years. It has been studied for several hundred years—most recently using high-powered electronic equipment—but still no one can claim to understand it fully.

POLTERGEIST ACTIVITY

An ordinary ghost can be terrifying, but a poltergeist can also be dangerous because it has physical power. Its name comes from the German *poltern*, which means "to create a disturbance," and *geist*, which means "ghost." A poltergeist is always noisy and usually disruptive. It has kinetic energy—which means that it can move things around. It can throw heavy objects across a room, smash china and glass, and even throw stones that were not in the room in the first place. A poltergeist's activities can be triggered anywhere at any time, and unless they are stopped, they will build to a crescendo before dying down—and then perhaps starting all over again.

A very active poltergeist can destroy everything within its range, and people who are closeby may be hit with flying furniture or cut by pieces of broken china or glass.

DEMONS AND LITTLE PEOPLE

Some poltergeists are aggressive; others are just mischievous and no more than a nuisance. In the world of fantasy imps, demons, and goblins all have the ability to throw things and create chaos, and most of the Little People—if they feel annoyed or slighted— can also cause strange noises and upheavals.

PSYCHOKINETIC ENERGY

A poltergeist almost always focuses on one person in a household—and that person is usually, although not always, young. There is a possibility that the person central to the attacks may be causing them, accidentally or on purpose, using psychokinetic energy, or mind power.

LEY LINES

In 1921 Alfred Watkins, a respected merchant and amateur archaeologist, noticed that stone circles, standing stones, megalithic tombs, churches built on ancient sacred sites, and beacon hills appeared to be placed in straight lines across the British countryside. He named these lines "ley lines" and assumed that they marked prehistoric trading routes. It is possible, though, that they also mark the currents of the earth's energy, which are recognized in other countries and which in China are called *lung-mei*, or dragon paths. Research shows that poltergeist activity often occurs on ley lines, especially where ley lines cross each other.

POLTERGEISTS IN BOOKS AND MOVIES

📖 *Eustace*
Catherine Jinks

📖 *The Ghost of Thomas Kempe*
Penelope Lively

📖 *Harry Potter and the Sorcerer's Stone*
J. K. Rowling

🎬 *The Haunted Mansion* (2003)

🎬 *Ghostbusters* (1984)

Ghost ships and eerie beasts

Fully rigged sailing ships that come into view and then melt away and vanish, horses that emerge out of the night but are not really there, fierce black dogs that disappear as suddenly as they appear—all of these have been reported over the years, often by reliable witnesses. Some have been explained away as time slip or place memory (see page 129) or as mirages or other tricks of the light. Others remain mysterious.

In Norse mythology Fenrir the Fenris Wolf is a vast and aggressive creature. The gods protected themselves and the world by tying him down with a magic chain, from which he will not break free until the end of the world.

THE FLYING DUTCHMAN

The most famous of many phantom ships is known as *The Flying Dutchman*—although in fact "Dutchman" refers to the captain, not to the ship. It is a 17th-century two-masted brigantine, a Dutch merchant vessel. There are several legends attached to her that have been told in books, a movie, and an opera by Wagner. All agree that she ran into trouble in a storm off the Cape of Good Hope, South Africa. Most say that her captain refused to turn back but swore to Heaven and the devil that he would sail around the cape if he had to sail until Doomsday. So the ghostly ship, with her crew of corpses and skeletons, sails on forever, a chilling omen of doom. Among those said to have seen her are a young midshipman in the Royal Navy, who was to become King George V of Great Britain, and the crew of a World War II German U-boat.

St. Elmo's Fire may account for some of the sightings of ghostly looking ships. This is a shimmering blue light that dances on the masts and superstructure of ships after electrical storms.

The Barguest mostly occurs in northern Great Britain. It is a terrible creature that haunts dark lanes and churchyards, most often in the form of a giant dog with eyes like burning coals, although it can shape-shift into a cat or a goblin.

THE DOGS OF DEATH

Many cultures connect dogs—whose association with humans goes back thousands of years—with death. They may guard the entrance to the underworld, like Cerberus, or guide the spirits of the dead, like Syama and Sabala (see pages 68–69). In many cultures spectral black dogs are linked with individual families—and the sight of one heralds the death of a family member, in much the same way as the cry of the banshee. Ghostly hounds have been sighted on many lonely paths at night, especially in Great Britain and other Celtic lands, usually alone but occasionally hunting in packs. Even if they do not bring death they certainly arouse great fear.

Almost all animals are aware of the presence of ghosts and supernatural beings, but horses—long regarded as sacred animals—are especially sensitive. Most people who ride or work with them know that a horse can be "spooked" by something that no one else can see.

The Wild Hunt

On winter nights of storm and fury in the Celtic lands of northern Europe the Wild and Savage Hunt can be heard—and may be glimpsed—streaming across the skies. The hooves of their phantom horses make the sound of thunder; their spectral hounds howl in the wind. The thousands of riders are the dead and the undead, seeking the souls of the damned. Sometimes the frenzied horses are black, accompanied by wild-eyed, jet-black hounds. Sometimes the horses are as pale as death and the red-eared hounds are as white as snow. The fearsome hunt may be led by Odin or Woden, the Norse god of death and magic, or by a spirit huntsman, or by the devil himself. If the huntsman is Gwyn ap Nuad, the Welsh god of war and death, the hounds are only three in number—one white, one black, and one bloodred. Mortal dogs may howl as the hunt streams by, but mortal men and women should beware of looking at it for fear of being swept away.

The Wild Hunt in Books

☐ *The Dark is Rising*
Susan Cooper

☐ *The Moon of Gomrath*
Alan Garner

☐ *Count Karlstein*
Philip Pullman

☐ *The Wild Hunt*
Jane Yolen

List of creatures by area

Some of the fantastic creatures and beings within this book are known almost everywhere. But some seem to only enter our own world in specific countries or on specific continents. Certain magicians and monsters were born and lived (or still live) in one location. It is these that are listed here.

ARCTIC CIRCLE

uldra *Little People* (page 25)

GREENLAND:

Margyr *mythical being* (page 85)

AFRICA

camelopard *mysterious animal* (page 43)
werecrocodiles *shape-shifters* (page 108)

EGYPT:

Great Sphinx *mythical being* (page 79)
Hermes Trismegistus *wizard* (page 99)
mummies *the undead* (page 118)

SOUTH AFRICA:

Flying Dutchman *ghosts and spirits* (page 132)
Tokoloshi *Little People* (page 23)

THE AMERICAS

NORTH AMERICA:

bogeyman *Little People* (page 23)
Bokwus *nature spirit* (page 37)
Ogopogo (N'haitaka) *mysterious animal* Canada (pages 46–47)
Sasquatch (bigfoot) *mysterious animal* (page 45)
Slimy Slim *mysterious animal* U.S. (page 46)
thunderbird *fabulous beast* (page 63)
Windigo *mythical being* (page 83)

CENTRAL AMERICA:

Quetzalcoatl *god and fabulous beast* (page 62)

SOUTH AMERICA:

Ahuitzotl *nature spirit* (page 38)
werejaguars *shape-shifters* (page 108)

ASIA

Arabian phoenix *fabulous beast* (page 61)
genies or **djinn** *ghosts and spirits* (pages 122–123)
ghûls *shape-shifting demons* (page 126)
griffins *fabulous beasts* (pages 60–61)
Nagas and **Nagini** *gods and fabulous beasts* (page 67)
roc *fabulous beast* (page 63)
yeti (abominable snowman) *mysterious animal* (page 44)

CHINA:

Chinese dragon *fabulous beasts* (page 52)
Feng-Hwang *fabulous beasts* (page 61)
Ki Lin (Ch'i Lin) *fabulous beasts* (page 56)
weresnake *shape-shifter* (page 108)
Yellow Dragon *fabulous beasts* (page 53)

INDIA:

garuda bird *fabulous beast* (page 62)

manticore *mysterious animal* (page 42)
Syama the Black and **Sabala the Spotted** *fabulous beasts* (page 69)
weretigers *shape-shifters* (page 108)

INDONESIA:

Rangda *witch goddess* (page 93)

JAPAN:

Ho-o *fabulous beasts* (page 61)
Issie *mysterious animal* (page 46)
Japanese dragons *fabulous beasts* (page 52)
Kirin *fabulous beasts* (pages 56)
Ningyo *mythical being* (page 85)
vampire cat of Nabeshima *the undead* (page 112)

KOREA:

Korean dragons *fabulous beasts* (page 52)
dokkaebi *ghost* (page 128)

EUROPE

basilisk *fabulous animal* (page 65)
bluecaps *Little People* (page 24)
bogeymen *Little People* (page 23)
cockatrice *fabulous animal* (page 65)
doppelgängers *ghosts and spirits* (page 125)
ghouls *the undead* (page 126)
golems *clay monsters* (page 119)
Green Man *nature spirit* (page 37)
Hippogriff *fabulous beasts* (page 61)
Morgan le Fay *enchantress* (page 93)

rusalka *nature spirit* (page 38)
Western dragons *fabulous beasts*
  (pages 54–55)
Western unicorns *fabulous beasts*
  (pages 56–57)
wyvern *fabulous beast* (page 64)

NORTHERN EUROPE:

barbegazi *Little People* (page 25)
thumpers or **knockers** *Little People*
  (page 24)
uldra *Little People* (page 25)

EASTERN EUROPE:

vodyanoi *nature spirit* (page 38)

GREAT BRITAIN:

Barguest *ghost dog* (page 133)
boggarts *Little People* (page 23)
brownies *Little People* (page 20)
corpse-light *phantom lights* (page 41)
fox fire *phantom lights* (page 41)
Gwydion *magician* (page 99)
Herne the Hunter *nature spirit* (page 36)
hobgoblins *Little People* (page 20)
ignis fatuus *phantom lights* (page 41)
Jack O'Lantern *phantom lights* (page 41)
John Dee *magician and alchemist* (page 98)
kelpie *nature spirit* (page 39)
Merlin *wizard* (page 98)
Nessie, the Loch Ness monster
  mysterious animal (page 47)
piskies *Little People* (page 20)
pixies *Little People* (page 15)
Robin Goodfellow (Puck) *Little People*
  (page 18)
screaming skulls *the undead* (page 116)
seal women *mythical beings* (page 87)
selkies *mythical beings* (page 87)
trows *mythical beings* (page 83)
Will O'The Wisp *phantom lights* (page 41)

CZECH REPEBLIC:

Bubak *Little People* (page 23)

THE NETHERLANDS:

redcaps *Little People* (page 20)

FRANCE:

White Ladies *Little People* (page 23)

GERMANY:

Boggelman *Little People* (page 23)
Elberich, Dwarf King *Little People*
  (page 18)
Erl King *Little People* (page 22)
kobolds *Little People* (page 21)
nixes *nature spirits* (page 38)
wichtlein *Little People* (page 24)

CLASSICAL GREECE AND ROME:

Atlas *mythical being* (page 80)
centaurs *mythical beings* (page 76)
Cerberus *fabulous beast* (page 68)
Charybdis *mythical being* (page 73)
Chimera *fabulous beast* (page 64)
Circe *enchantress* (page 92)
Cyclops *mythical beings* (page 82)
Dryads *nature spirits* (page 32)
fauns *nature spirits* (page 34)
Furies *mythical beings* (page 74)
Gorgons *mythical beings* (page 74)
Hamadryads *nature spirits* (page 32)
Harpies *mythical beings* (page 75)
Hecate *witch and goddess* (page 93)
Hermes Trismegistus *wizard* (page 99)
hippocampus *mythical being* (page 85)
Hydra *fabulous beast* (page 66)
Janus *god* (page 68)
Minotaur *mythical being* (page 77)
Muses *mythical beings* (pages 70–71)
Neptune *god* (page 84)
Nereids *nature spirits* (page 33)
nymphs *nature spirits* (page 32)
Oceanids *nature spirits* (page 33)
Oracles *mythical beings* (page 78)
Pan *god* (page 36)
Pegasus *mythical beings* (page 59)
Poseidon *god* (page 84)
satyrs *nature spirits* (page 34)
Scylla *mythical being* (page 73)
Sirens *mythical beings* (page 72)
Sphinx of Thebes *mythical being* (page 79)
Titans *mythical beings* (page 80)
Tritons *mythical beings* (page 85)

ICELAND:

ninnir *nature spirits* (page 39)

IRELAND:

Bocan *Little People* (page 23)

fetch *ghost* (page 124)
leprechauns *Little People* (page 15)
Morrigan *goddess, shape-shifter* (page 125)
pooka *nature spirit* (page 40)

ROMANIA:

Count Dracula *the undead* (page 115)

RUSSIA:

Alsvid the Allswift *fabulous beasts*
  (page 58)
Arvak the Early Riser *fabulous beasts*
  (page 58)
Asilky *mythical beings* (page 81)
Baba Yaga *witch* (page 93)
domovoy *Little People* (page 21)
leshies *nature spirits* (page 35)

SCANDINAVIA:

Fenrir the Fenris Wolf *mythical beast*
  (page 132)
frost giants *mythical beings* (page 81)
Garm *fabulous beast* (page 69)
Heimdall *god* (page 68)
kraken *mysterious animal* (page 49)
necks *nature spirits* (page 39)
nis *Little People* (page 20)
Nornir or **Norns** *Little People* (page 19)
trolls *mythical beings* (page 83)

OCEANIA & AUSTRALIA

AUSTRALIA:

bunyip *nature spirit or mysterious beast*
  (page 39)
mimis *nature spirits*
  (page 41)
werecrocodiles *shape-shifters* (page 108)

NEW ZEALAND:

Patu-Paiarehe *Little People*
  (page 15)

Glossary

aggressive Hostile, warlike, and liable to attack, either with words or weapons.

ancestors Great-grandparents, their parents, and so on, all the way back to the distant past.

avengers Those who take revenge, often on behalf of others.

Aztecs Native American people who built a great empire in Mexico from the A.D. 1300s until it was conquered by the Spanish in the 1500s.

barrows Ancient burial mounds.

benevolent Friendly, kindly, or helpful.

billabongs Small rivers or parts of rivers that come to a dead end; stagnant pools.

cannibal A person or animal who eats the flesh of its own kind.

carrion Dead and rotten flesh.

celestial Of the sky or the heavens.

composite Made up of several different parts.

constellation A group of stars whose shape, when seen from the earth, seems to form the outline of beings or animals.

decomposing Decaying or rotting.

demons Evil spirits, devils.

destiny Fate—a future that has been planned in advance by the gods or some other power.

deterrent Anything that persuades someone against a certain course of action.

divine Like the gods, or coming from the gods, or God Himself.

dugong A large, air-breathing sea mammal related to the manatee. Both are sometimes called sea cows.

eerie Weird and frightening.

effigy Something made to look like, or represent, a person or god. An effigy may be made of almost any material, including stone, metal, or clay.

elixir A liquid mixture used to turn ordinary metal into gold or as a medicine to give unusually long life to a patient.

emblem A symbol, symbolic image, or picture of something.

enchantment A type of magic.

eternity Forever and ever—time without end.

ethereal Light and delicate.

executed Killed as a result of a sentence of death.

exposure To be uncovered or unprotected.

extinct Died out and no longer in existence.

fables Stories, sometimes supernatural, often with animal characters, told in order to teach a moral lesson. The word is sometimes used for myths and legends.

faery An ancient word for fairyland; also used to describe a being or a creature that comes from fairyland.

ferocious Fierce and dangerous.

folklore The traditional beliefs of a people or a culture, often containing memories of things that have actually happened in the distant past.

ford A part of a river or stream where the water is shallow enough for people, animals, carts, or cars to cross.

foretell To tell about something before it has happened.

fossilized Preserved by nature in ice or dry sand or turned into stone inside ancient rock. Fossilized remains are usually skeletons, or parts of skeletons, or plants—sometimes only the shape of the once-living creature or plant has been saved.

gauzy Being so thin and transparent that it is possible to see through to the other side.

gnarled Twisted and knobbly, like an old tree.

Gothic Gothic novels, such as Bram Stoker's *Dracula*, are always full of mystery, strange happenings, and horror.

heraldry The decorations, symbols, and colors used to represent a person, a family, or a ruler and his or her descendants. Originally used on banners, standards, and shields so that people could recognize each other in battle. Now used more widely, especially by cities and businesses.

hibernate To sleep through the winter.

hoard A supply or collection of something.

hoaxes Fakes, imitations of a real thing, tricks, or practical jokes.

humanity The human race.

immortal Living forever, never dying.

imperial Of an empire or emperor; royal.

instinctive Doing something by instinct, without thought or planning.

iridescent Glowing with rainbow colors, something that changes color as it moves.

labyrinth A maze; pathways or passages that twist and turn, many leading to dead ends.

lance A weapon with a long wooden handle and a pointed tip.

legends Traditional stories, usually about a specific person or place. The word is sometimes used for myths and fables. Originally all these stories were spoken and not written down. They were told by professional or amateur storytellers or passed down through families and changed a little with each telling.

macabre Gruesome.

malicious Cruel, wanting to hurt and do harm.

martyr A person who suffers for his or her religious faith or beliefs, and who is sometimes tortured or killed for refusing to give up these beliefs.

medieval Refers to the Middle Ages in Europe, from the A.D. 400s to the middle of the 1400s.

meteorites Small pieces of rock or metal that fall to the earth from outer space without burning up in the atmosphere. Meteorites that burn up and briefly glow in the night sky are called shooting stars.

mirages Optical illusions, things seen that are not really there.

mortal A human being who will eventually die, like all humans.

myths Traditional stories, often about large subjects—the lives of gods and goddesses and the creation of this and other worlds. Many myths explain human behavior and natural events such as earthquakes. The word is sometimes used for fables and legends.

navigation Finding the way, steering a ship, an aircraft, etc., on the right course.

navigator A person who is trained in navigation.

nourishing Giving energy and sustaining or supporting life. Usually used when talking about food.

occult To do with the supernatural and with mystical and magical knowledge.

omens Things that happen, or are seen, and are thought to predict the future.

outwitted To outwit someone, you need to be more clever and crafty than they are.

pagan Not part of any of the main religions of the world, often following ancient beliefs and nature worship. Pagan does not mean Satanic or evil.

pestilence and plague Names for any type of terrible disease that spreads rapidly and almost always kills its victims.

plectrum A small piece of horn, ivory, metal, or plastic used to pluck the strings of a musical instrument such as a guitar or a lute.

plesiosaurs Extinct dinosaurs with long necks and flippers that once lived in seas and lakes.

plumage The feathers of birds.

pollution Anything that makes the air, water, or earth filthy such as oil spills or smoke or gas pouring into the air.

provisions Food, water, milk, and other supplies.

psychic Psychic events or happenings are mysterious and magical and cannot be explained or understood easily; a psychic is a person with occult powers.

putrid Rotten, rotted away, smelly, and slimy.

realms Kingdoms, areas in the control of one ruler or group of rulers.

resurrection The return to life of someone who has died; rising up from the dead.

revelations The revealing of knowledge; glimpses of the future or of great truths.

rituals Ceremonial acts.

sacrificed Killed and offered to a god or gods.

shamans People who form a link between this world and the world of spirits. Sometimes a type of priest.

shape-shift The ability to change from one shape into another—from a man into a wolf, for example.

shrine A sacred place that is often decorated with sacred objects or pictures, where a god or saint is worshipped.

sonar Often used to search for things that are underwater; sound is sent out, and its returning echoes are recorded on a screen, showing the shape of invisible, underwater objects.

standards Flags or banners with colors, patterns, or images that are easy to recognize and that represent a person or a group—a monarch, a kingdom, an army regiment, or a noble family.

summons An order to appear.

supernatural Outside the normal laws of nature, mystical or magical; used of gods, ghosts, and fairies, among others.

tempests Very bad storms with strong winds.

treacherous Not to be trusted, dangerous.

tribute A gift given to show respect.

U-boat A German submarine used in World War I and World War II.

vengeful Looking for vengeance or revenge.

venom A liquid poison produced by snakes and other reptiles and injected into a victim with a bite or a sting.

vigorous Strong and energetic.

visions Things seen in the imagination or in dreams or trances.

voodoo A religion mostly practiced in the Caribbean, especially Haiti.

wraith Ghost of a dead person.

Index

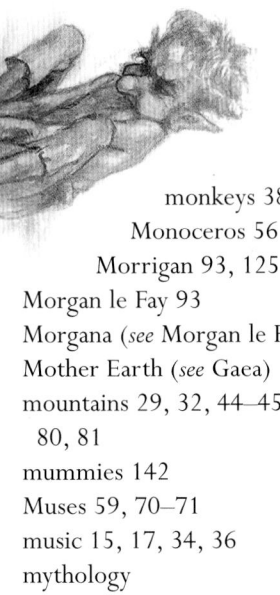

Acknowledgments

The publisher would like to thank the following for permission to reproduce their material. Every care has been taken to trace copyright holders. However, if there have been unintentional omissions or failure to trace copyright holders, we apologize and will, if informed, endeavor to make corrections in any future edition.

Key: *b* = bottom, *c* = center, *l* = left, *r* = right, *t* = top

Cover: *front cover* Mark Turner/www.enchanted.co.uk/photography by Mark Eager/Runic Design; *cover flaps* Patricia Ludlow/Linden Artists; *back cover l* Topfoto; *back cover c* Popperfoto; *back cover r* Bridgeman Art Library (BAL)/The Marsden Archive

Pages: 1 Corbis/Elizabeth Whiting; 1*c* Corbis/State Russian Museum; 1*c* Corbis/Todd Gipstein; 1*c* Patricia Ludlow/Linden Artists; 2–3 John Howe/Arena; 4–5 John Howe/Arena; 5*tl* David Goode/www.david-goode.com;6–7 Richard Hook/Linden Artists; 10–11 Nicki Palin; 12–13 British Museum; 14 John Howe/Arena; 15*cl* BAL/Victoria & Albert Museum; 15*cr* Patricia Ludlow/Linden Artists; 16 Patricia Ludlow/Linden Artists; 17*tl* Corbis; 17*tl* Corbis/Buddy Mays; 17*c* Mary Evans Picture Library (MEPL); 18*tl* MEPL; 18*br* Topfoto; 19 BAL/Private Collection; 20 David Goode; 21*t* MEPL; 21*c* Patricia Ludlow/Linden Artists; 21*b* Patricia Ludlow/Linden Artists; 22*t* BAL/Fairy Art Museum, Tokyo; 22*b* David Goode; 22–23*c* Getty Imagebank; 23*tr* BAL/Private Collection; 24*tl* MEPL; 25 Richard Hook/Linden Artists; 26 David Goode; 27*b* Getty Hulton; 28–29 John Howe/Arena; 30 Corbis/Andrea Wells; 30*bl* Corbis/Christie's Images; 30–31 Corbis; 31*tr* Getty Imagebank; 32–33 Nicki Palin; 34*tl* Art Archive/Victoria & Albert Museum; 34*b* Topfoto; 35*bl* Getty Stone; 35*r* John Howe/Arena; 36*tl* BAL/ Private Collection; 36*bl* Topfoto; 36–37 John Howe/Arena; 38*cr* Werner Forman Archive; 38*bl* BAL/Private Collection; 39 Corbis/Corcoran Gallery of Art; 40*tl* Corbis; 40*r* Alamy; 41*tr* Mary Evans Picture Library; 41*cl* Getty Imagebank; 42–43 Richard Hook/Linden Artists; 44–45*t* Getty NGS; 44–45*b* Getty NGS; 44*t* Topfoto/Fortean; 44 Topfoto; 45*r* Lee Gibbons; 45*tr* Corbis/Darrell Guilin; 45*tr* Topfoto; 46 Popperfoto; 46–47 Patricia Ludlow/Linden Artists; 48–49 John Howe/Arena; 49 BAL/Fitzwilliam Museum, Cambridge; 50–51 John Howe/Arena; 52*tl* Corbis/Charles and Josette Lenars; 52–53 Corbis/Philadelphia Museum of Art; 54*tl* Corbis/Reuters; 54–55 John Howe/Arena; 55*tr* Corbis/National Gallery, London; 56*t* Kunsthistorische Museum, Vienna; 56*b* BAL/Musee National du Moyen Age, Cluny; 57 Nicki Palin; 58 Patricia Ludlow/Linden Artists; 59 BAL/Neue Pinatothek, Munich; 60–61 Getty Imagebank; 60–61 Corbis/Kevin Schaeffer; 60*b* Corbis/Araldo de Luca; 62*b* Corbis/Christie's Images; 62–63*t* Patricia Ludlow/Linden Artists; 63*b* Corbis; 64–65 Corbis Elio Ciol; 65*t* Nicki Palin; 66*br* BAL/Musee Gustave Moreau, Paris; 67 Corbis/Luca Tettoni; 68–69 Corbis/Tim Davis; 69 Art Archive/British Museum; 70–71 Scala/Vatican; 72*cl* BAL/National Gallery, Melbourne; 72–73 Getty Imagebank; 73*cl* Alamy; 73*tr* AKG, London; 74*bl* AKG, London; 74–75*c* Corbis/Araldo de Luca; 75*r* BAL/Felix Labisse Collection, France; 76 John Howe/Arena; 77*tl* BAL/Heraklion Museum, Crete; 77*br* Art Archive/Biblioteca Estense Modena/Dagli Orti; 78*tl* AKG, London; 78*bl* Alamy; 79 Corbis/Christie's Images; 80–81 Getty/RHPL; 80*tl* Art Archive/Real Biblioteca de lo Escorial/Dagli Orti; 80*br* Corbis; 81*tr* Mary Evans Picture Library; 82*l* BAL/Museum of Fine Arts, Boston; 82*lc* Corbis/Michael Prince; 83*cl* Natural History Museum, London; 83*tr* BAL/National Museum, Stockholm; 84–85 Michael Embden/Arena; 85*tl* BAL/Musee Conde, France; 87*tr* Topfoto; 88–89 John Howe/Arena; 90*bc* Alamy; 91*tr* AKG London; 91*b* John Howe/Arena; 92 John Howe/Arena; 93*tl* BAL; 93*cr* Werner Forman Archive; 94–95 BAL/Private Collection; 95*tr* BAL/Private Collection; 96*cl* BAL/de Morgan Centre, London; 96*br* BPK, Berlin/States Museum, Berlin; 97*c* Corbis; 97*br* Art Archive; 98 Julek Heller/Arena; 99*t* Topfoto; 99*c* Getty Imagebank; 100 Dominic Harman/Arena; 100–101*t* Art Archive/Dagli Orti; 100–101*b* Topfoto; 102–103 Corbis/Elizabeth Whiting; 102–103 Corbis/Russian State Museum; 103*tr* Getty Stone; 103*cr* Getty Photodisc Green; 104–105 Art Archive/Dagli Orti; 104*tl* Corbis/Gianni Dagli Orti; 104*cl, cr* Werner Forman Archive; 105*b* Science Photo Library; 106–107 Richard Hook/Linden Artists; 108–109 Getty Imagebank; 108*br* Topfoto; 110 Richard Hook/Linden Artists; 112*tl* Frank Lane Picture Agency; 112–113*b* Terry Oakes/Arena; 113*cl* Getty Imagebank; 113*cr* Getty Photodisc Green; 114–115 BAL/Marsden; 114*b* Les Edwards/Arena; 115*t* BAL; 116–117 British Museum; 116*b* British Museum; 117*c* Art Archive/Mexico City Museum; 117*b* British Museum; 118 Nicki Palin; 120–121 Dominic Harman/Arena; 122*l* BAL/Royal Watercolour Society; 123*c* Corbis/Hermann/Starke; 124*l* BAL/Musee d'Orsay; 125 Photolibrary.com/OSF; 126*tl* Getty Imagebank; 126*b* Getty Stone; 127*tl* BAL/Stavropol Museum, Russia; 127*cr* BAL/Detroit Institute of Arts; 128*r* Corbis/Olivier Martel; 128–129 Corbis/Sandro Vannini; 129*t* Corbis/Elizabeth Opalenik; 130*b* Corbis; 130–131*t* Corbis/Sandford Agliolo; 131*c* Photolibrary.com/OSF; 131*tr* Mary Evans Picture Library; 132–133 Corbis; 132*cl* Werner Forman Archive; 132–133 Corbis/Joseph Sohm; 133*t* Julek Heller/Arena; 134–135 BAL/Gavin Graham Gallery; 138 Corbis/Christie's Images; 140 Mary Evans Picture Library; 141 British Museum; Patricia Ludlow/Linden Artists; 143 Nicki Palin

The book and movie icons for the book panels on each spread: Encompass Graphics

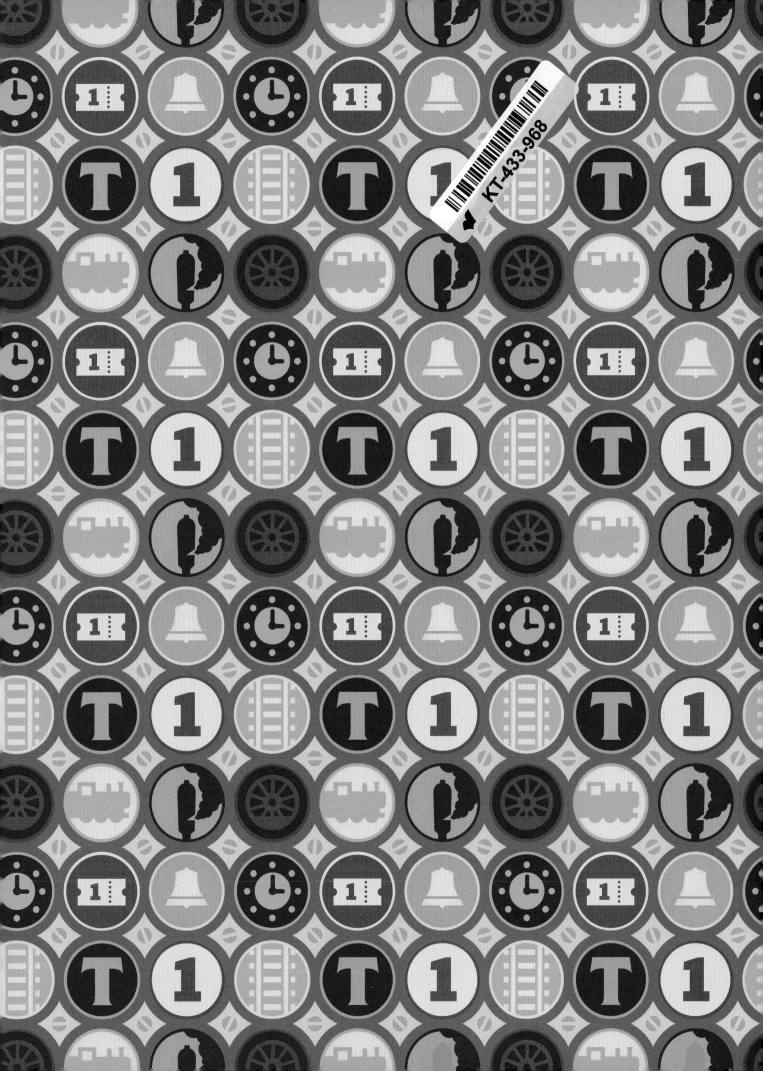

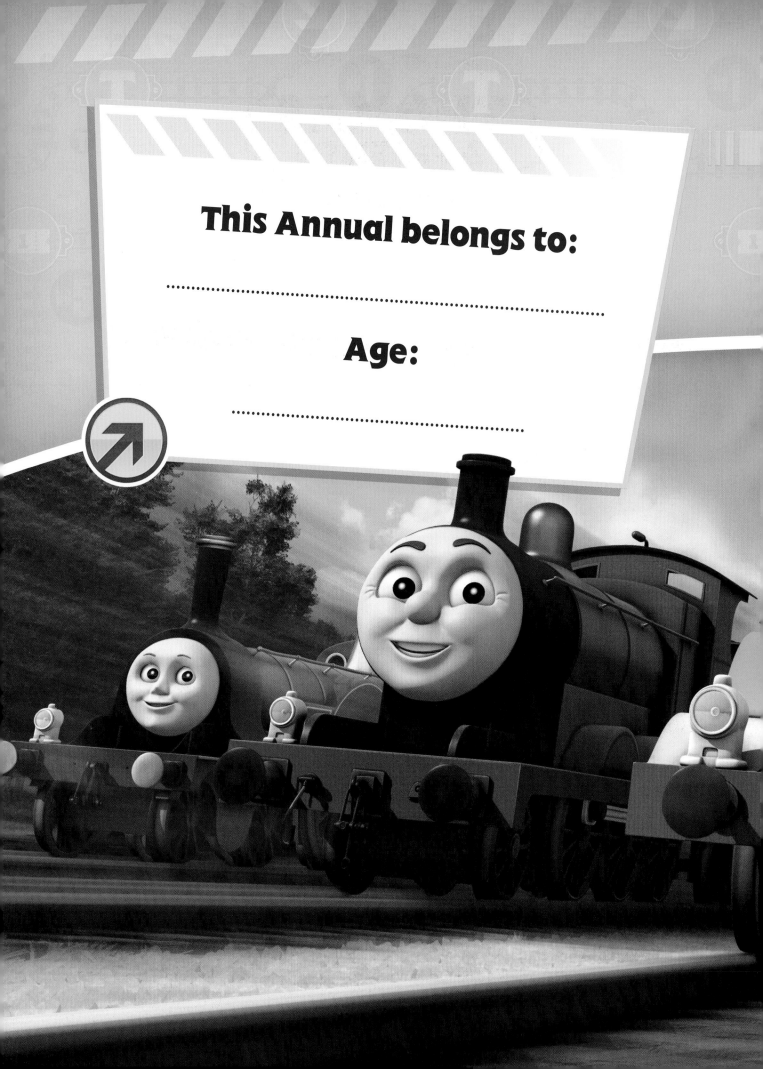

This Annual belongs to:

....

Age:

....

THOMAS & FRIENDS™

My favourite engine is:

....

Annual 2018

EGMONT
We bring stories to life

First published in Great Britain in 2017 by Egmont UK Limited
The Yellow Building, 1 Nicholas Road, London W11 4AN

Written by Mara Alperin
Designed by Elaine Wilkinson and Martin Aggett

Thomas the Tank Engine & Friends™

HiT entertainment   C R E A T E D   B Y   B R I T T   A L L C R O F T

ISBN 978 1 4052 8755 5
67223/1

Printed in Italy

Contents

Meet the Steam Team

1 Thomas

Thomas is number 1.
He loves taking passengers around Sodor on his very own Branch Line!

2 Edward

Edward is number 2.
He is very wise and one of the oldest engines on Sodor.

3 Henry

Henry is number 3.
He is proud of his green paint and loves going really fast on the Main Line.

4 Gordon

Gordon is number 4.
This big Express Engine is the fastest engine in the Steam Team.

5 James

James is number 5.
He loves pulling coaches
but he hates taking the
Troublesome Trucks!

6 Percy

Percy is number 6.
He is a small green engine who
loves pulling the Mail Train.

7 Toby

Toby is number 7.
He works hard on the Quarry
Line with his coach, Henrietta.

Emily

Emily is a green engine.
She is kind-hearted and always
helps out those in need.

Engine Shed Spotting

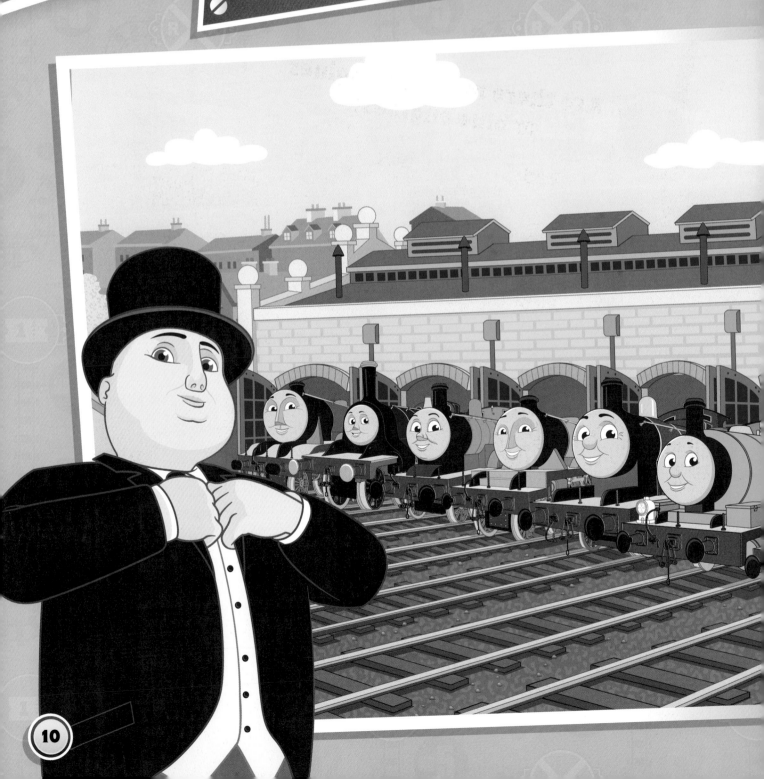

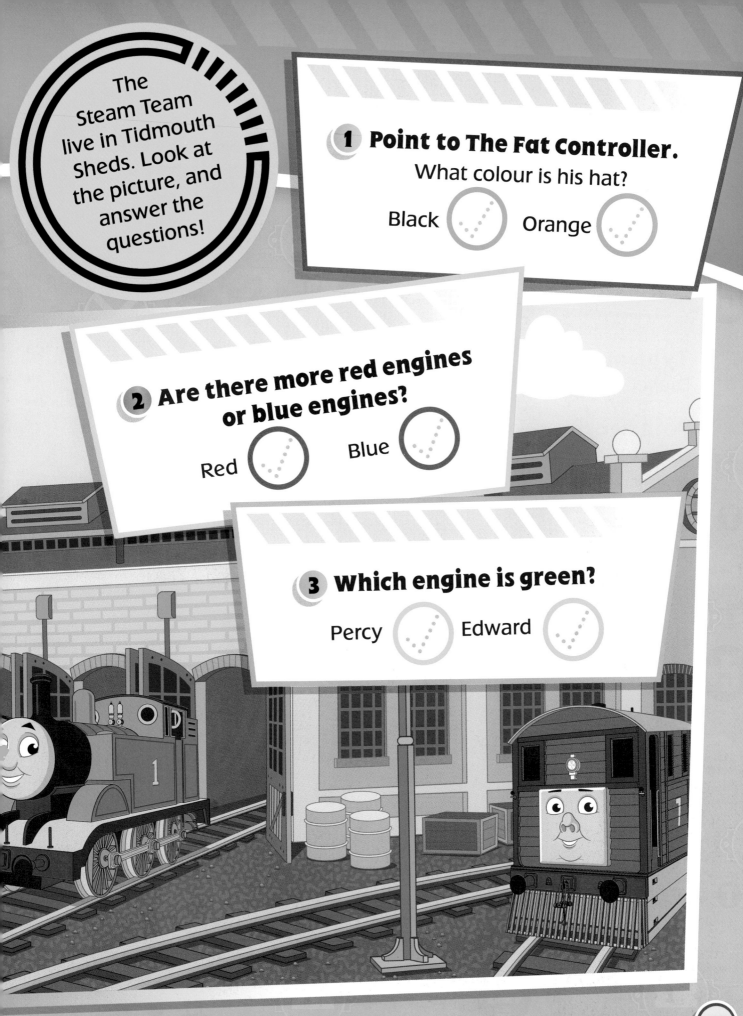

The Steam Team live in Tidmouth Sheds. Look at the picture, and answer the questions!

1 Point to The Fat Controller.
What colour is his hat?

Black ◯   Orange ✓

2 Are there more red engines or blue engines?

Red ✓   Blue ✓

3 Which engine is green?

Percy ✓   Edward ✓

Answers on page 68.

Meet Sidney

→

Really Useful Facts about Sidney

Type of engine:
Diesel engine

Paintwork:
Dark blue with yellow lining

Features:
Sidney has a striped warning panel underneath his face.

Fun fact:
Sidney is very kind and likes to help his friends, but he can be a bit forgetful!

I'm a very helpful engine!

Sidney is a diesel engine. Circle another diesel engine.

Henry

Diesel

HELLO!

Sidney is a very friendly engine. He likes to help his friends. Name something you do that is helpful.

One Christmas, the Diesels decorated Sidney in twinkling lights.

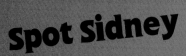

Spot Sidney

Which picture is Sidney in? Tick the right picture.

a

b

c

Sodor Steamworks

Knapford Station

Sodor Clay Pits

Answers on page 68.

Sidney Sings

Sidney was a **very helpful engine**. But he was also a **very forgetful engine**.

Sometimes, he forgot where he was going and what he needed to do!

One day, The Fat Controller gave Sidney a very important job. *"I want you to **collect Percy's new wheels from Brendam Docks** and take them to the Steamworks."*

Sidney didn't want to let his friends down.
But **he was worried** that he might forget something.
So Sidney made up a **little song** to help him remember:

Ha ha ha, hee hee hee.
A very special job for me.
All the way to Brendam Docks,
To fetch a very special box!

Now Sidney was sure that **he wouldn't forget** where he was going or what he was supposed to collect.

Then Sidney saw Gordon up ahead. *"Hello, Gordon!"* he called, as his friend whooshed past.

Oh, no! Speaking to Gordon had made Sidney forget the words to his song. And so this time he sang:

♪ *Ha ha ha. Hee hee hee.*
A very special job for me.
All the way to Whiff's Waste Dump.
To fetch a boiler or a pump!

"Hello, Whiff!" Sidney said when he arrived at Whiff's Waste Dump.

"Hello, Sidney. What are you doing here?" Whiff asked.

Sidney had already **forgotten!**

"It's a shame you're not an elephant," said Whiff. *"Elephants never forget."*

"Elephants!" gasped Sidney. **"Maybe that's what my special job was!"** He sang his remembering song again:

♪ *Ha ha ha. Hee hee hee.*
A very special job for me.
I must get there before it's dark
To collect an elephant from the Animal Park!

Sidney rushed over to Sodor Animal Park, but he didn't see any elephants. **"Oh dear,"** he said. *"I must have got it wrong again."*

Sidney drove away sadly. On the way home, he noticed a queue of passengers at Knapford Station.

"Excuse me," said one of the passengers. *"We have to catch our cruise ship, but our train hasn't arrived to take us to Brendam Docks."*

"That must be my special job!" cried Sidney. He sang his remembering song one more time:

> *Ha ha ha. Hee hee hee.*
> *A very special job for me.*
> *These people are going on a trip,*
> *And I'm taking them to catch their ship!*

So the passengers climbed aboard and Sidney raced along the tracks to Brendam Docks.

Meanwhile, **The Fat Controller was worried.** He had been waiting for hours at Brendam Docks, but Sidney hadn't arrived to pick up Percy's wheels. *"Where could Sidney be?"* he wondered.

Then Sidney pulled up with the coach of passengers.

"Thank you, thank you!" all the passengers called, as they headed off to catch their ship. *"You were a very useful engine, Sidney!"*

The Fat Controller was pleased that Sidney had helped the passengers. But Percy's wheels still needed to be delivered.

"You mean you have another special job for me?" Sidney said. He had completely forgotten his first job! **"I'd be delighted to take these wheels to Percy!"**

Sidney wrote a new song to help him remember:

Ha ha ha. Hee hee hee.
Another special job for me.
On me you know you can depend,
I'm going to the Steamworks to see my friend!

Poor Percy had been waiting all day for his new wheels. He was very relieved when Sidney finally pulled up to the Steamworks.

"Here I am!" Sidney said. *"I've brought your new wheels. You didn't think that I'd forget now, did you?"*

The End.

Story Quiz

How well do you remember the story **Sidney Sings**?

Tick the correct answer to each question!

1 What did The Fat Controller ask Sidney to collect from Brendam Docks?

a. a new boiler ◯

b. Percy's new wheels ◯

c. an elephant ◯

2 Who did Sidney come across on his way?

a. Bertie ◯

b. Diesel ◯

c. Gordon ◯

3 What did Sidney do to try and remember his special job?

a. sing a song about it ◯

b. write it down ◯

c. ask The Fat Controller to remind him ◯

Answers on page 68.

20

Jigsaw Jumble

The Search and Rescue team are ready to go!

Which jigsaw piece is missing from this picture?

a

b

c

Answer on page 68.

Spot the Difference

Colour in a train each time you find a difference!

Can you spot all five differences in the big picture?

Answers on page 68.

Percy and the Sheep

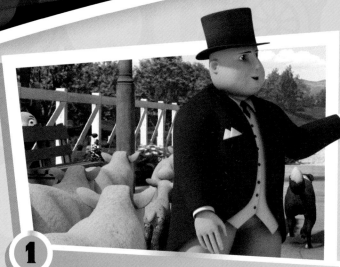

1 The Fat Controller asks Percy to take Farmer McColl's sheep to the Spring Fair.

2 "Don't worry, Sir," says Percy.

3 But Percy doesn't notice that there is a hole in the back of the carriage!

4 Every time he stops, a sheep hops out of the carriage and onto the tracks.

5 Luckily, Thomas is right behind Percy. He stops to collect all the sheep.

6 They ride in his coach Annie, next to his passengers.

7 Farmer McColl is happy to have all his sheep back.

8 "Thank you for helping me, Thomas!" Percy says. "I promise to be more careful next time."

Counting

Sheep

Help Thomas pick up the lost sheep as fast as possible by following the tracks.

Start

Finish

How many sheep did you find?

can you make a sound like a sheep?

Baa! Baa!

26

Answer on page 68.

Day at the Seaside

Answers on page 68.

James is off to the beach.

Circle the items you think his passengers will need. Then colour them in!

Dot-to-Dot

Connect the dots to finish off Bertie the Bus.

1
2
3
21
20
4
5

7
6
8

Toot! Toot!

19
18
17

11
10
12
9

14
13
16 15

Colour him in with your brightest red crayon!

Draw a big tick next to Bertie's passengers.

a

pigs

b

people

28

Bus Tour

Bertie picks up passengers all over the Island of Sodor.

Trace the path with your finger, and count the bus stops along the way!

Start

1

2

3

4

5

Finish

Say Toot! Toot! to let people know that Bertie is here!

Answers on page 68.

Are there more people at stop **1** or stop **5**?

How many people are at stop **4**?

There are ☐ stops.

Meet Caitlin

I love to race!

Really Useful Facts about Caitlin

Type of engine:
Steam engine

Paintwork:
Pink with light blue lining

Features: Caitlin has a set of coaches that match her paintwork.

Job:
Caitlin works for the Earl of Sodor, transporting passengers to and from Ulfstead Castle.

Fun fact:
Caitlin is a very speedy engine. She loves racing her friend Connor!

WHOOSH!

Caitlin is a very fast engine. Can you think of something else that's very fast?

Caitlin races her friend Connor!

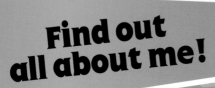

Find out all about me!

Does Caitlin have blue stripes or blue spots?

Who does Caitlin work for?
a. The Duke of Boxford.
b. The Earl of Sodor.

Answers on page 68.

Best Engine Ever

Read the story about Caitlin the steam engine. Listen to the words and join in when you see a picture!

Caitlin

Emily

Victor

Thomas

 is a very fast steam engine. One day,

is racing along when she sees  stuck on the track.

"Hello ," says . "I've broken down

and I can't move."

"Everyone breaks down sometimes," replies.

So zooms to the Steamworks

for repairs. is very impressed because

is so fast! At the Steamworks, mends .

"I wish I could be fast like ," says sadly.

But tells that speed isn't everything.

"  is right," agrees. "You are a great

engine just the way you are." The next day,

needs help. Her brakes have failed, and she can't stop!

"Don't worry, ! I can help!"  cries bravely.

 crashes into , but holds her brakes

on, and soon both and come safely to a stop.

"Thank you for saving me," tells .

This time, it's who takes to at the

Steamworks. Now realises that both she and

can be Really Useful – and very good friends!

All About You

Emily and Caitlin are both very good at different things! What are some of the things you do best?

Tick as many as you like!

Having tea parties

Splashing in puddles

Singing

Jumping

Flying a kite

Sharing with my friends

Playing hide-and-seek

Painting pictures

Building forts

Doing puzzles

Building towers with blocks

Sharing my toys

Playing I Spy

Building snowmen

Dancing

Running

Being kind to animals

Collecting rocks

Dressing up

Picking flowers

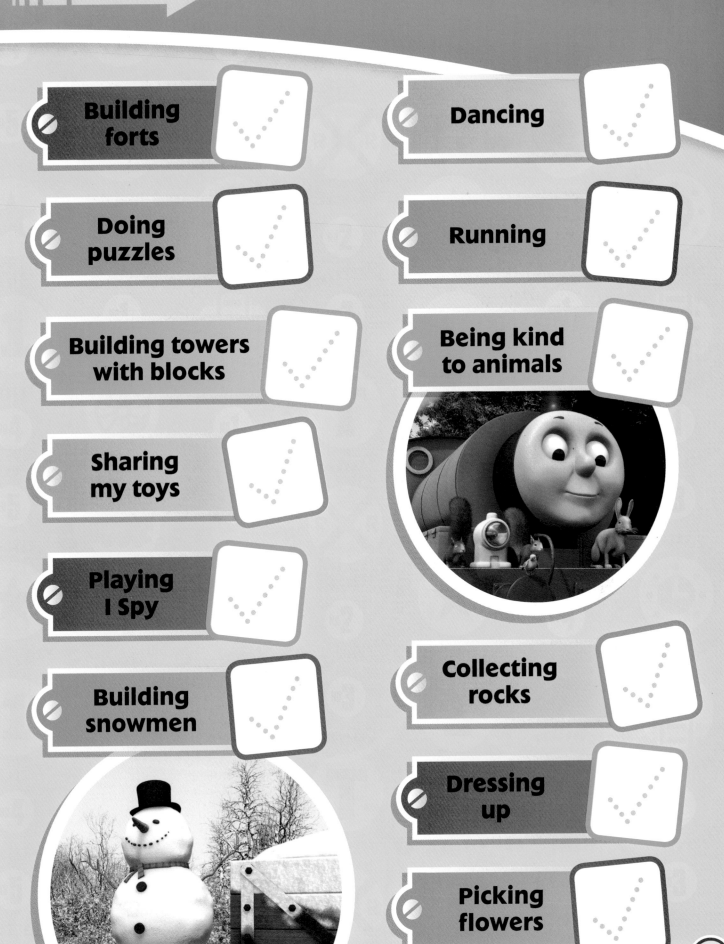

Thomas

Colouring

Colour in this picture of Thomas, using the small picture as a guide.

Thomas is a blue engine. Tick another blue engine!

 **a**

 **b**

Answer on page 68.

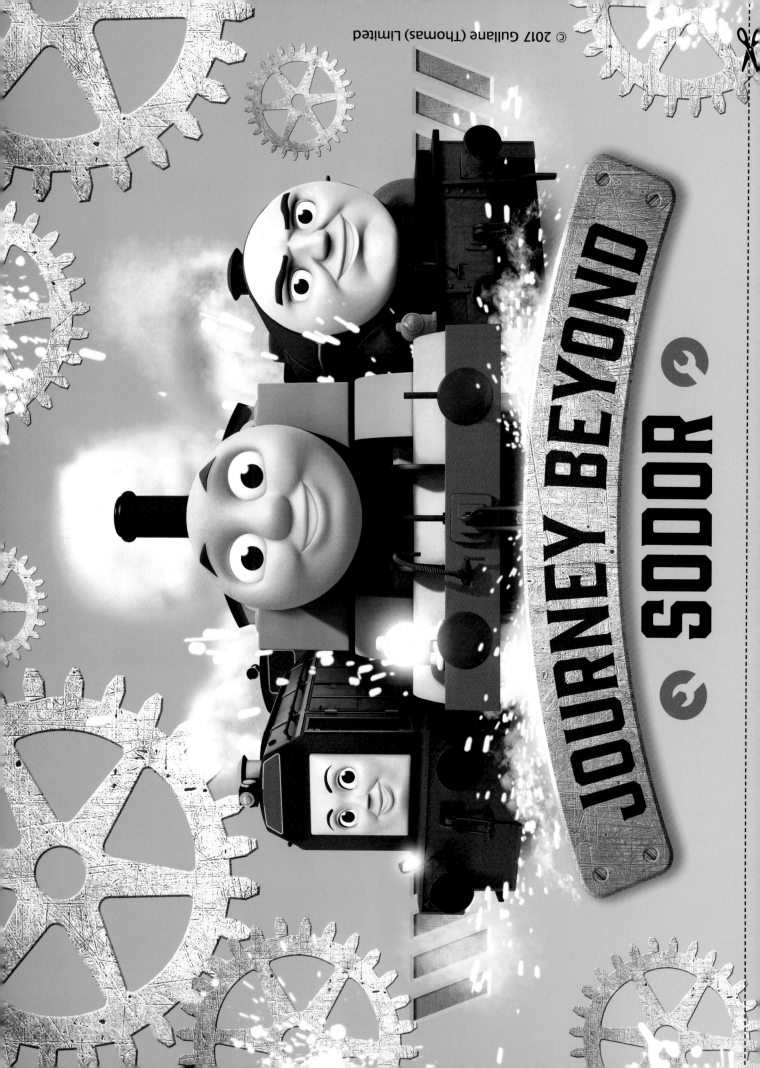

JOURNEY BEYOND

SODOR

Whizz around with Thomas as he journeys beyond Sodor.

Use your finger to follow the track from start to finish!

Hello, I'm Frankie!

What colour are the flags?

Hello, I'm Hurricane!

Finish

Hello, I'm Theo!

What an adventure!

The Whale Rescue

1 One hot summer's day, a whale is stranded on the beach in Sodor!

2 The Sodor Search and Rescue team rush over to the beach together.

3 Belle sprays the whale with water to keep her cool.

4 Rocky the Rescue Crane hoists the whale onto Oliver's flatbed.

5 Oliver takes the whale to Brendam Docks, where the water is deeper.

6 Cranky carefully lowers the whale back into the water.

Splash!

7 Now the whale can swim safely back to her home.

8 Thomas cheers for the whale… and for the Search and Rescue Team!

Search and Rescue
Spotter

The Search and Rescue Team work together to save the day!

Can you spot these smaller pictures in the big one?
Tick each one as you find them.

a

b

c

Now match each rescue engine to its shadow!

Answers on page 68.

Henry Glows in the Dark

Read the story about Henry's new coat of paint. Listen to the words and join in when you see a picture!

Henry  **Thomas**  **Kevin**  **The Fat Controller**  **paint**

One day, went to Sodor Steamworks to be repainted.

He was very excited about getting a new, shiny green coat

of  ! At the Steamworks,  was very busy.

He was painting signs with special glow-in-the-dark ,

48

so the engines could see them at night. Poor got

confused, and he painted with the glow-in-the-dark

 instead! At first, didn't notice the difference.

But as the sun went down, something strange happened.

 began to glow.

"**Ahhhhhhh**! It's a ghost engine!" gasped ,

and he chuffed away to the Sheds as quickly as he could.

"There's no such thing as a ghost engine,"

told . Then he turned around and saw .

"**Ahhhhhhh**!" cried  . "It's only me," said .

"Of course,"  coughed. "  must have painted

you with the wrong kind of . You'll need to be

repainted in the morning." "Yes, sir," replied.

"I'd rather be a proper green engine than a glow-in-the-dark

engine any day!"

Henry

Colouring

Colour Henry in with your brightest green crayon!

Kevin forgot that Henry needs a new coat of green paint. Can you help him?

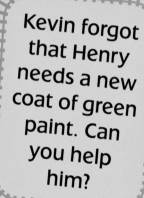

What number engine is Henry? Trace the number here.

3

Counting

Cargo

The engines deliver lots of different cargo.

Use the number line below to count how many carriages or flatbeds each engine has.

a

MILK + MILK + MILK + MILK + [1] =

b

OIL + OIL + OIL + [2] =

c

Sodor Mail + Sodor Mail + [6] =

1 2 3 4 5 6 7 8 9 10

Meet Glynn

Really Useful Facts about Glynn

Type of engine:
Boiler engine

Paintwork:
Red with gold lining

Features: Glynn has a yellow number one painted on his side ... just like Thomas!

Fun fact:
Glynn worked on Thomas' Branch Line before Thomas arrived. Now Glynn works at Ulfstead Castle.

Being Useful makes me feel good!

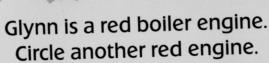

Glynn is a red boiler engine.
Circle another red engine.

Hiro

James

Fa la la la!

Scrub! Scrub! Glynn gets cleaned up at the Steamworks!

One Christmas, Glynn took The Fat Controller to a party at Ulfstead Castle. What do you like to do at Christmas?

what is the weather like?

Glynn drives carefully down the tracks. What is the weather in the picture? Tick the right answer!

a **Rainy** ◯

b **Sunny** ◯

c **Snowy** ◯

Answers on page 68.

55

The Christmas Coffeepot

It was **nearly Christmas**, and Marion the Steam Shovel was working on Thomas' Branch Line.

As **Marion dug snow away** to clear the tracks, she saw a face hidden in the branches. And then the face started to speak!

"It's a talking Christmas tree!" Marion gasped.

"Wait," the voice replied. *"I'm not a talking tree."*

But **Marion didn't listen**. She hurried off to tell her friends about the talking tree.

"Are you sure?" asked Thomas and Percy.

"You must go and have a look," said Marion.

So Thomas and Percy went to **see for themselves.**

Thomas and Percy drove down the tracks until they found where Marion had been digging. Their Drivers cleared away the branches, and suddenly they saw what Marion had found!

"This isn't a talking Christmas tree," said Percy.

"You're right," Thomas replied. *"This is Glynn, the Coffeepot Engine who used to run my Branch Line."*

Glynn was glad to see Thomas and Percy.
But he was feeling rather sad – he wished that he could be a useful engine again!

"I expect The Fat Controller will take me to the Scrap Yard now," Glynn said with a sigh.

Thomas and Percy were worried about Glynn.
How could they help him become a Useful Engine again?

"Glynn is old, but Stephen is even older," Percy said thoughtfully. *"And Stephen is still working up at Ulfstead Castle."*

"That's brilliant!" Thomas cheered. *"We can take Glynn to the Earl at Ulfstead Castle!"*

So the next morning Thomas went back to find Glynn, and this time he brought the Earl with him.

"Glynn is a very special engine indeed!" the Earl agreed. And he arranged for Glynn to be taken to the Sodor Steamworks to be restored.

"Thank you, Sir," said Glynn. And he thanked Thomas, Percy and Marion too!

Soon, **The Fat Controller arrived** at the Sodor Steamworks. At first, Thomas and Percy were worried that The Fat Controller would be angry. But The Fat Controller just smiled.

"This is a marvellous idea!" he said. *"I'm only sorry I didn't think of it myself!"*

Then The Fat Controller asked Glynn to take him to the **Earl's Christmas party.**

"Of course, Sir!" Glynn said happily. *"It will be just like old times!"*

Later that evening, the engines gathered at Ulfstead Castle for the Christmas party.

"Another engine working at the Castle is the best present I could have wished for," the Earl declared.

"Merry Christmas, everyone!"

Thomas Craft

You will need:

- Scissors
- Thin card
- Glue
- Cargo for Thomas' flatbeds

1 Cut along the scissor line on the side of the next page.

2 Glue the page onto a piece of thin cardboard. Leave to dry.

3 Cut along the dotted lines to cut our Thomas and his flatbeds.

4 Use your imagination to load Thomas' flatbeds!

Here are some cargo ideas:

- stickers • crayons • paints • buttons • leaves or feathers
- rocks or shells • toothpicks • cotton balls • uncooked pasta

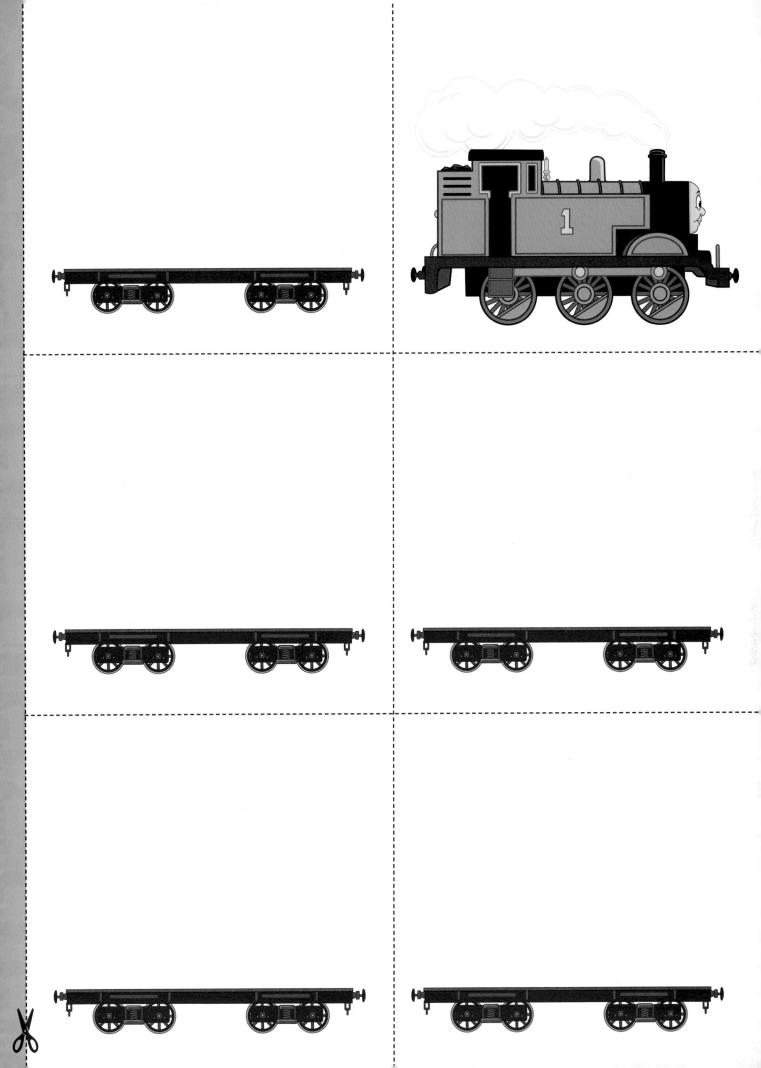

Cranky's Game

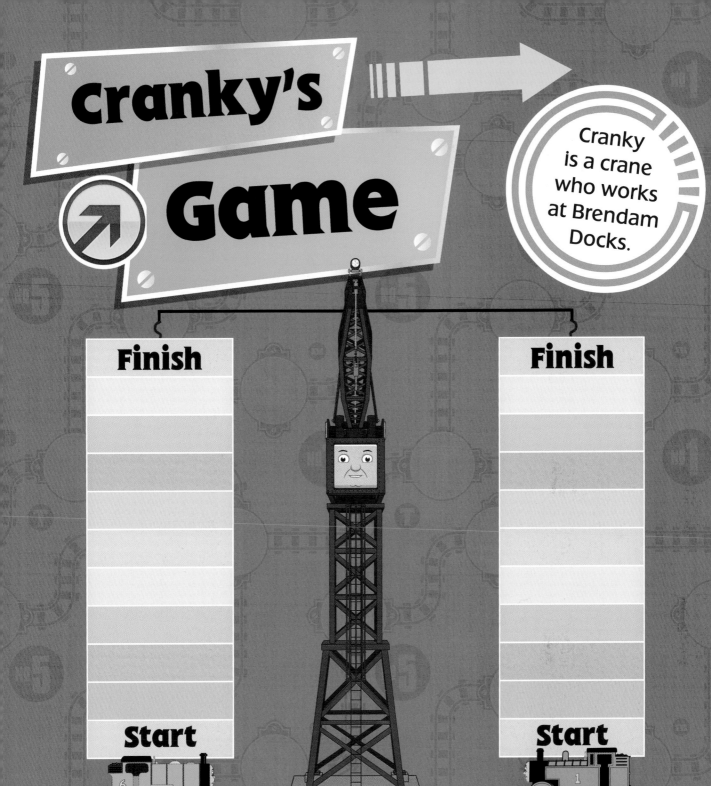

Cranky is a crane who works at Brendam Docks.

Finish

Start

Finish

Start

Play Cranky's Game and help him lift Thomas and Percy!

HOW TO PLAY:

· Decide who will be Thomas and who will be Percy
· Place a counter or button on your START
· On your turn throw a coin and see how it lands. If it lands heads up, move 2 spaces up. If it lands tails up, move 1 space down.
· The first one to reach FINISH is the winner!

Missing Shape Match

Can you match up the missing pieces of Thomas and his friends?

Use the shapes to help you.

a

b

c

d

e

CRANKY

Answers on page 68.

Thomas All Year Round

1 **What season do you think it is?**

Spring ✓   Autumn ✓

2 **What is Thomas carrying in his flatbed?**

Apples ✓   Pumpkins ✓

3 **What colour is the scarecrow's coat?**

Blue ✓   Purple ✓

Look at these pictures of Thomas, and answer the questions below!

1 What season do you think it is?

Summer Winter

2 What holiday are the engines celebrating?

Christmas ✓ Easter

3 How many presents can you count under the tree?

Three Four

Answers on page 68.

Answers

Pages 10-11
1. Black 2. Blue 3. Percy

Pages 12-13
Diesel is a diesel engine.
b. Knapford Station

Page 20
1. b 2. c 3. a

Page 21
c

Pages 22-23

Page 26
There are 8 sheep.

Page 27
James' passengers will need the bucket and spade, sunglasses and beachball.

Page 28
b. People

Page 29
There are more people at stop 5.
There are 3 people at stop 4.
There are 5 stops.

Page 31
Caitlin has blue stripes.
b. The Earl of Sodor

Page 38
b. Edward

Page 41

Pages 42-43
Thomas passes 2 windmills.
The flags are red.

Page 47

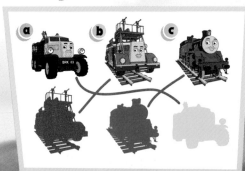

Page 53
a. 4 **b.** 3 **c.** 2

Page 54
James is a red engine.

Page 55
c. Snowy

Pages 64-65

Page 66
1. Autumn
2. Pumpkins
3. Blue

Page 67
1. Winter
2. Christmas
3. There are four presents under the tree.

№1 №5 №6
RIGHT ON TIME
1

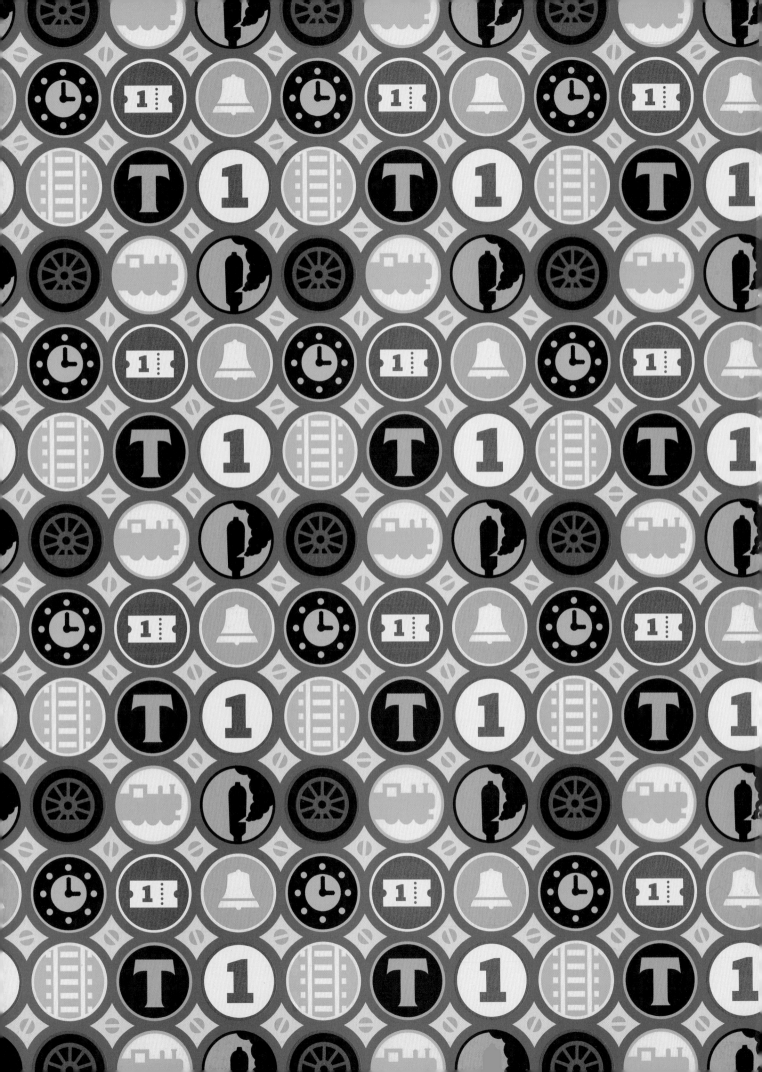